The Great Indian
SCHOOL
BAZAAR

Dev takes us on a deeply personal journey through the complex changing terrain of our educational space. This acutely observed account is insightful and illuminating as he tackles complex issues and questions that, as educators, we have continued to grapple with over decades. In our conflicted times, he makes an intense plea for equity, access and acceptance. He affirms the faith that every educator has about the future—if we have hope—it is because of our children. His message is needed now more than ever, as the values many of us believe in, stood for and fought for, come under renewed attack.

Thank you, Dev!

—Abha Adams, educationist

In my humble opinion, this is fascinating Bible Study material for teachers, parents and students graduating from school into the joy and wonders of lives thereafter. It thrills, shocks and, while you like it all, you are often confronted by truths we selfishly sweep under our rugs—for personal or societal 'convenience'. Testaments penned by a great educationist whose unbiased intellect and compassionate heart are in perfect harmony to stimulate those who wish to open their minds and eyes to what education really ought to mean. Dev Lahiri's little diary is archive material for posterity to dwell upon.

—Victor Banerjee, film and theatre artiste

People hanker after good education for their children. What is good education? Where is it available? Why is it not more common? This daring little book attempts to answer these questions. It combines a dedicated teacher's insights with a school administrator's analysis of the current scenario. It explains why education is more complex than what people realize. Dev Lahiri persuades us to view education in terms of life at school, or rather, how a child might experience the life a school offers. The range of issues Dev Lahiri deals with is vast, but you don't feel that he is simplifying anything. On the contrary, you admire his patience with questions that you didn't want to face yourself.

—Krishna Kumar, Padma Shri awardee and former Director, National Council of Educational Research and Training (NCERT)

Dev Lahiri captures the institution of schooling in India with a delightful turn of phrase. While humour is sprinkled all through the writing, Lahiri's wit is acerbic. From the aspirations of parents, members of school managements and miscellaneous hangers-on to the bewilderment of teachers and students, he captures the many shades of conflict and collaboration that make up day-to-day life in school. Rather than a mere description of passing moments, he delves deeper, giving his distinctive perspective on issues as diverse as value education, teacher selection and school leadership. This book fills the gap between academic writing about Indian schools and journalistic reports. These lived experiences of a schoolmaster not only hold up a mirror to a faltering school system but also draw attention to contemporary institutionalization of education.

—Sonali Nag, Associate Professor of Education and the Developing Child, University of Oxford (UK) and Honorary Associate Director, The Promise Foundation (India)

The Great Indian School Bazaar is an excellent analysis of the problems, prospects, and potential of the Indian school education system. With sharp insight and much-needed honesty, Dev Lahiri draws upon decades of experience to articulate where we are, and where we need to be, in our efforts to bequeath our children the future they deserve. His writing spans the breadth of our education system without compromising on depth, enlightening readers on issues ranging from leadership and sports to bullying and rote-learning. His anecdotes make evident that this book is a product of a lifelong commitment towards this most noble of causes, reflecting a wealth of both personal observations and diverse interactions. Free from moralistic undertones, it offers those working to develop young minds a reason to hope and those seeking to build a progressive India a plan of action. The book appears at a time that most urgently demands it, and I recommend it warmly to educators, policymakers and students alike.

—Shashi Tharoor, Member of Parliament for Thiruvananthapuram

The Great Indian
SCHOOL
BAZAAR

Travels through the World of Education

DEV LAHIRI

Published by
Rupa Publications India Pvt. Ltd 2018
7/16, Ansari Road, Daryaganj
New Delhi 110002

Sales centres:
Allahabad Bengaluru Chennai
Hyderabad Jaipur Kathmandu
Kolkata Mumbai

Copyright © Dev Lahiri 2018

The views and opinions expressed in this book are the author's own and the facts are as reported by him which have been verified to the extent possible, and the publishers are not in any way liable for the same.

All rights reserved.
No part of this publication may be reproduced, transmitted, or stored in a retrieval system, in any form or by any means, electronic, mechanical, photocopying, recording or otherwise, without the prior permission of the publisher.

ISBN: 978-93-5304-359-9

First impression 2018

10 9 8 7 6 5 4 3 2 1

The moral right of the author has been asserted.

Printed by HT Media Ltd, Gr. Noida

This book is sold subject to the condition that it shall not, by way of trade or otherwise, be lent, resold, hired out, or otherwise circulated, without the publisher's prior consent, in any form of binding or cover other than that in which it is published.

*To my late father, Lt Col Debaprasad Lahiri,
who taught me one of life's most important lessons:
There can be no greater evil than 'sitting on the fence.'*

Contents

Foreword	*xi*
Preface	*xv*
1. Why School?	1
2. What about Values?	11
3. The Scourge of Bullying	27
4. The Leadership and Management of Schools	35
5. Fun and Games	53
6. Where Are We Heading?	61
7. From Cocoon to Butterfly	80
8. The Problem of Principals	91
9. Of This and That	98
10. Of Schools, Parents and Children	109
11. The Lighter Side	126
12. Reflections of a Teacher	136
Acknowledgements	149

Foreword

Lewis Carroll, the pseudonym used by mathematician Charles Dodgson, wrote the endearing book, *Alice's Adventures in Wonderland*, in 1865. The story is about a girl who disappears down a rabbit hole to a fantastical place and goes through bizarre adventures. In one sequence, Alice has this conversation with the Cheshire Cat:

> 'But I don't want to go among mad people,' Alice remarked.
> 'Oh, you can't help that,' said the Cat, 'we're all mad here. I'm mad. You're mad.'
> 'How do you know I am mad?' asked Alice.
> 'You must be,' said the Cat, 'or you wouldn't have come here.'

Dev Lahiri has ventured into the 'mad world' of Indian school education. To the purists, I apologize in advance if my use of the word, 'mad' offends them. I don't intend to underestimate the importance of the subject! Reading Dev Lahiri's book about the dilemmas of Indian school education just happened to remind me of Alice's story. The author admits that the subject is complex and multilayered and, with modesty, he writes that he is no expert on it.

The fact remains that he has been a grounded and sensitively observant schoolteacher for forty years—above all, he became a schoolteacher because he *wanted* to become one, in preference to staying in a corporate job. I am aware that he joined my previous company, Hindustan Lever, many years ago as a manager, but quit to teach.

The subject of schools and education is vast and complex; and there are many scholarly (and unreadable) reports about the state of the Indian education system. But what this hugely experienced schoolteacher has attempted to do here is to write, through the narratives of his own experience, the slimmest and, arguably, the most readable book on the subject. He states that he did not set out to be prescriptive, but rather share anecdotes that illustrate the issues and choices that face us—as parents, as a society and as people who are vitally interested in the well-being of future generations.

Dev Lahiri insists that school education issues and leadership are quite different from the other worlds—for instance, business. As I read his manuscript, I wonder whether he is quite right. As someone who has spent fifty years in the corporate sector, I could relate to his description of the several dilemmas that he has faced.

For example, who is the 'customer' of the school service? The student who is being educated? The parent who is paying the fees? The teachers who are engaged in what could be a thankless job? The alumni of the school? (My definition of alumni is that they are the former students who are convinced that the school reached its apogee during their time in the school.) Or, the community at large?

Well, in corporate speak, all of them are stakeholders. Each of them has a valid interest in the effectiveness of the school. The only trouble is that they have different flight paths to reach the same goal of becoming—and staying—excellent.

Ultimately, just as in corporates, the board has to spend quality time in developing and selecting the principal or headmaster, agreeing on broad school goals with him or her and then, leaving the principal alone. As it happens in corporations, promoters and boards know this, but are reluctant to practise the tenet in real life. Schools are no different! Promoters and boards must learn the art of influence, but should not confuse it with interference—in schools and in companies.

I am delighted that Dev Lahiri has written this book, and I feel that every parent should read it and think about the issues raised by him in his narratives. If that happens, his efforts will not have been in vain.

R. Gopalakrishnan,
Author and Corporate Adviser
3 December 2017

Preface

This little book in no way pretends to be a comprehensive study of the Indian education system. That system is far too complex and multilayered to lend itself to such an evaluation, particularly by lesser mortals like me.

Yet, allow me to illustrate the gigantic dimensions of the issues confronting education in this country. This is perhaps best done by Vikram Patel, the Pershing Square Professor of Global Health at Harvard Medical School, in his incisive article[1] in *The Indian Express*. Patel writes:

> The latest report of the Annual Survey of Education, published last year, and based on assessments of basic abilities of reading, writing, and arithmetic of over five lakh rural children, offered a glimpse into the scale of the challenge confronting India. While 95 percent of children aged 6 to 11 years were enrolled in schools, a large proportion of children were simply not learning. Nationally, less than half the children in class 3 were able to read a class[1] text, a figure which had shown virtually no improvement since 2011. One out of every four children

---

[1] Patel, Vikram, 'Our Best Investment', *The Indian Express*, 13 August 2017; http://indianexpress.com/article/opinion/columns/our-best-investment-right-of-children-to-free-and-compulsory-education-in-india/

enrolled in class 8 could not read at class 2 levels. Just over a quarter of class 3 children could do a two-digit subtraction and a similar proportion of class 5 children could do simple division.

Even grimmer is what Patel goes on to say:

> What is also clear from these figures is that a huge proportion of India's children exceeding 50 million in a recent estimate, experiences fundamental limitations of learning abilities which have their roots well before they even enter primary school. In short, their intellectual capabilities, a direct outcome of the level of cognitive development of the brain have been deprived by enormous deprivations in the early years of their lives.

This is a frightening scenario; and as someone who is rooted in an urban culture and having dealt only with schools where the middle and upper middle classes send their children, I would not even dare to begin to explore the issues raised in this article. It is my fond hope, however, that someone with much greater knowledge and experience of this sector will indeed put it all together so that it becomes public knowledge, rather than just being reading material for a privileged few.

What this book does do, however, is attempt to map out my journey over some well-charted and some not-so-well-charted areas in our world of education (and by that I mean the urban middle class educational experience), much in the nature of a travelogue. I have attempted, in these few pages, to try and highlight—faithfully—some of the experiences I have had, and the lessons that I have learnt from them.

At no point can I claim that I have found all the answers. As a matter of fact, many readers will perhaps discern errors in my analyses of situations and my responses to them. I, for one, would be very happy if that were to happen, because it would mean that I would have achieved at least one of the objectives I had set for myself when I began writing these chapters—to encourage people to at least think about some of the problems that seem to bedevil our education system. For I am convinced that education is far too sensitive and important a subject to be left to 'expert planners' in some isolated office. All stakeholders need to be involved. After all, what is at stake is our greatest legacy—the future of our children and, indeed, of our country.

Dev Lahiri

1

Why School?

One of the greatest aspirations of people whom we seem to encounter in everyday life, is to provide what they consider, a 'good education' to their children. Of course opinions differ on what constitutes a 'good education', as indeed do the motives for wanting to provide one. For some, it is a fancy air-conditioned (AC) school with AC buses. For others, it is a boarding school of old repute. For many, it is a school that promotes 'traditional values', and for others, one that prepares their child for a foreign university. If you speak to your auto-driver on this issue, he is more than likely to say, '*Hamein to bacche ko angrezi school bhejna hai*' (I want to send my child to an 'English-medium' school). To get their children out of the vicious cycle of poverty is a powerful motive for many. The recent film, *Hindi Medium*, illustrates, albeit in a somewhat exaggerated manner as films must do, the desperation parents feel in order to secure admission to a school of their choice.

And not in all cases is the driving force just a desire to provide a good education that will ensure a prosperous future for the child. Some parents are obsessed with the idea of admission to a particular school only in order to 'keep up with the Joneses'. For others, it signifies a move up on the social ladder. I saw this happen in a big way in the Doon valley in the '80s. This was largely on account of the presence in the Doon valley of the famous Doon School, founded in 1935, and widely regarded as the 'mother of all public schools'. The popularity of this 'Doon syndrome' perhaps reached its peak in 1985, when, during the Golden Jubilee celebrations of the school, the nation suddenly woke up to the fact that the then Prime Minister—Rajiv Gandhi—was its alumnus.

Rajiv Gandhi was then the glittering star, the role model for every upwardly mobile middle-class Indian. What happened during those years was that the distinction between sending your son to the Doon School and sending him to the Doon valley, became very blurred. After all, if you were to say in some parts of the country, '*Mera beta Doon mein padta hai*' (My son studies in Doon), who was to know the difference? Touts and auto-drivers at the railway station had a field day, escorting prospective candidates and their parents on a guided tour of the town's schools in their quest for the holy grail!

As a new teacher in the Doon School, it was interesting to see the impact it had on one's status. When travelling second class by train (which is what one could afford in those days), if a fellow passenger were to ask, 'What is it that you do for a living?' my answer, 'I am a schoolteacher', would most often be greeted by a stony silence or at best a grunt. If, however, some curious soul followed up by asking, 'Which school?' the answer, 'Doon school', would mean that one would be veritably mobbed by hordes of questioners, seeking information on admission procedures, fees and, of course, the great Indian question—'Will "pull" help?'

Then there are those parents who, despite being very affluent and successful in their line of work, would like their child to stay as far away from what they have been doing and take up something different altogether. Their choice of school is, therefore, coloured by that particular perspective. I have known army officers, doctors and lawyers say that this is 'the last thing that they wish for their child'. Perhaps they themselves have had a bad experience in their line of work, or feel that it holds no future for their child, which influences their perspective.

On the other hand, there is the opposite extreme, where a parent is determined that the child should follow in their footsteps, regardless of the child's aptitude or interests. I remember arguing for months with a father whose son was probably one of the finest artists I have encountered in my career, but who was determined that his son would have to be an engineer like him. All my pleas and arguments that a gifted artist such as his son could make a decent, and more importantly happy, living out of art fell on deaf ears. The son eventually spent almost seven years in order to qualify for engineering and is probably today a mediocre and unhappy engineer, when he could have been an excellent and well-to-do artist.

Against this backdrop, the story of 'R Sahib', as he was popularly known in his circles, is an unusual and interesting one. It so happened that as a young master at the Doon School, I was spending the Christmas vacation of 1986 with my family at my in-laws' place in Calcutta (now Kolkata). My great passion at the time was to exhibit my prize Doberman—'Bagheera'—at dog shows all over the country during the winter vacation. That year, the big show was in Kolkata, which fitted in nicely with my plans, though I daresay, perhaps not with that of my in-laws who would have to put up with an exceptionally large, boisterous, carnivorous beast in a modest flat for a month. My mother-in-law, I must admit, was particularly sporting about this issue. She, who could smell a dog even before one of its own species caught on and move rapidly in the opposite direction, actually consented to sharing the couch with this intruder whilst watching her favourite Bengali serial! What learned opinion Bagheera had to offer on the serial, I don't quite know, because I just did not have the courage to hang about under those circumstances. But if anyone deserved a gallantry award, I know it is my mother-in-law.

But, to return to the business of R Sahib and schools… One evening, a friend of mine, who was organizing the dog show that year and was a dog breeder of great repute in the city, visited me in a state of considerable frenzy.

'You have to do me a great favour,' he said. 'You have to come with me to visit R Sahib. He has sent you a special invite.'

'Who on earth is this person?' I asked.

'Don't worry about that now,' he said. 'Just know that my life will not be worth living if you refuse.'

Alarmed at the prospect of something untoward happening to my dear friend, I hastily boarded the pillion of his scooter and we headed towards North Calcutta. After negotiating some extremely tricky back alleys, we found ourselves in front of a stately, but ramshackle, old building, with some nondescript shops adorning the ground floor. What struck me immediately was that almost everyone around seemed to take note of our arrival, and I could have sworn that messages were exchanged through arched eyebrows, subtle nods and what-have-you. A rather swarthy individual then proceeded to escort us up the numerous flights of stairs. There were a number of apartments on each landing and I could hear music from sitars, tablas and harmoniums emanating from some of them, accompanied, at times, by the tinkle of ghungroos (ankle bells). Children played in the corridors on each floor.

Soon, we reached the topmost landing where there was only one door, guarded by two even swarthier individuals. They flung open the doors on our arrival and we were ushered into a rather large, well-lit hall. Does life imitate the movies or do movies imitate life? This was the question that sprung to mind as I took in what I was seeing. Seated at the end of the hall on a plush mattress were three bare-bodied men, and I could have sworn that the gentleman in the centre had walked off the sets of *Sholay*, the epic Hindi blockbuster. He was large, with a wide girth and pockmarked face and dressed in a lungi.

As soon as I entered, he burst into a loud greeting, '*Aaiye, master sahib, aaiye! Aap hee ki intizar thi*!' (Welcome, respected teacher! We were waiting for you only!) With that he signalled regally for us to take one of the low wicker chairs placed near the mattress. Gulping nervously, I lowered myself gingerly into the proffered seat, whilst my friend proceeded with the introductions. Sensing my unease, our Gabbar-like (Gabbar was the iconic villain in *Sholay*) host took over the proceedings.

'There is nothing to worry about,' he began, 'you are amongst friends,' (he had obviously noted the worried look on my face). To me, he sounded just about as reassuring as Colonel Sanders would do to a chicken. As the evening unfolded, so did the fascinating story of R Sahib.

R Sahib had come to Calcutta from Bihar as a young lad and started working in a dairy (which he eventually bought out). One thing led to another and he found himself in the 'muscle' business—providing protection to petty gang lords. It was a matter of time before he became one such 'lord' himself. Rivals were ruthlessly wiped out on the way and now he controlled all of North Calcutta. 'If there is a body floating down the Ganges, be sure that I know about it,' he told me proudly. 'But every woman and child is safe in my area,' he added for comfort.

Very soon drinks arrived. After the first round, R Sahib declared that we would adjourn to the terrace. There, a few empty beer bottles were placed on the parapet. R Sahib snapped his fingers and a flunky delivered a loaded revolver to him. Cool as a cucumber, R Sahib took careful aim and made short work of the bottles. By this time, the enormity of what I was getting involved in was beginning to sink in. I began to see a premature closure to my dreams of a distinguished career in education. Had R Sahib chosen me as his consigliere? Seeing the look on my face, and assuming that the pistol firing had frightened me, the don hastened to assure me, '*Fikar mat karein. Elaka hamara hai*' (Do not worry. The area belongs to me). Little did he know that I was imagining my whole future going up in smoke with his gunshots.

More was to follow. The bullets in the chamber exhausted—and my peace of mind shot to a sieve—we proceeded back to the chambers where dinner was ordered. While the table was being laid and flunkeys dispatched to fetch the juiciest kebabs and aromatic biryanis, R Sahib suddenly barked, '*Madam ko bulaiye*' (Bring in madam).

'Madam' swept in—in all her finery and bells jingling on her toes and ankles. She was, I was duly informed, the mistress of the notorious dacoit Madho Singh of the Chambal ravines, who was on the run from the police. She had turned to R Sahib, an old friend of the dacoit, for protection. And he had gladly provided it. Tonight, she was going to dance to entertain us. I had visions of someone filming the evening and sending a copy to my in-laws, and another to the Doon School! And as the lady danced, R Sahib drew out hundred-rupee notes from his pocket and showered her with largesse. I reached nervously for my wallet, dreading the embarrassment when I would pull out some measly small change, but the Don quickly put me at ease, saying I was his honoured guest for the evening. Little did he know how far away I wished to be from that honour!

During the dance, R Sahib explained to me that the entire building was inhabited by such dancers whom he considered his 'praja' (subjects). However, any customer who wished to do more than just watch a lady dance and sing would perforce have to marry her. If that code was violated, the offender ran the risk of never being able to propagate the species again!

As the evening drew to a close, R Sahib waved everyone out of the room and asked me to sit next to him. There was something intensely sad about the expression on his face. He looked a forlorn and tired man. 'You must be wondering what you are doing here in this company,' he said, as if reading my thoughts. 'You see, I have a ten-year-old son, and this is certainly not how I should be bringing him up. There have been two attempts on my life already. What kind of life is this for a young boy? I want him to make something completely different with his life.'

What R Sahib was almost begging me to do was to find a good boarding school for his son in Dehradun. I sat there stupefied. I had heard many parents wanting to put their son into a school—but never with this motive.

'Don't worry, take your time.' R Sahib, seeing the obvious consternation on my face, added, 'I know these things take time, and there are no guarantees. But do try and help. And, in the meanwhile, if there is ever anything I can do for you, do not hesitate to ask. *Yaad rakhna, Mughal badshah chale gaye par hum zinda hain*! (Remember, the Mughal rulers may have gone, but we are still around!)'

With these words ringing in my ears, I beat a hasty retreat from the strange and bizarre world of R Sahib. I must confess that I agonized long and hard about what I should do in the circumstances. One thing was clear. I was too low in the pecking order to be able to swing an admission, even if I so wanted. The most I could do was to provide information on the likely options. But the thought of any further embroilment in that world scared me stiff. So, I went back to Dehradun and put R Sahib out of my mind. Not quite, because the memory of that forlorn face desperately yearning for a different future for his son continued to haunt me. What a powerful force education could be! How many more young people like R Sahib's son could be shown a different path! And how many lives, in turn, that could impact!

As it happened, the next time I visited Calcutta, a few years later, R Sahib was no more. He had been shot in a gun battle with the police. The man left this world without fulfilling his dream of sending his son to 'Doon'. I have no idea of what his son has grown up to be. I can only hope that he has turned out to be the upright young man his father wanted him to be.

Having interacted closely with generations of parents and

children, it never ceases to amaze me when I see the range of expectations people have of the process of education. Very rarely, however (and sadly so) is it to let the children discover their potential and to go where their hearts lead them. Whilst I am aware that for those trapped in the vicious circle of poverty, such dreams are a luxury they cannot afford; what is dismaying is that even those who can afford to let their children follow their dreams, rarely do so.

Yet experience tells me that children, when given that freedom, very rarely fail. And even when they do (and that is not a bad thing), they learn to pick themselves up and have a go again. But we are so scared of failure ('What will the relatives and neighbours say?') and so obsessed with 'job security', that we will never dare to set them free. To a large extent, this is a fallout of a system where school-college-job form part of a watertight continuum, to break out of which is not an easy task. To remedy this, we will need a total re-look at the way in which we view school education, a point to which I will return in a different chapter.

This is why I am dismayed at the kind of counselling we have in our schools (that is, if we have it at all). Most counselling is focused on subject choices, which, in turn, is linked to career choices. Of course we must counsel our children. But we must counsel them about much bigger things, as for instance, how they can help make this world a better place. We must counsel them about making appropriate choices, not only in the matter of subjects, but in life, such as between right and wrong, justice and injustice, honesty and dishonesty.

And yes, we must counsel them about how to go about

assessing their own strengths and weaknesses, their own interests and passions, so that when the time comes, they will be able to make the appropriate choice of career, and not be afraid of 'failure' and experimentation. But school is not the time to make a career choice. School is a time for joyous exploration, for discovering the world in which they live, for asking awkward questions. School is only a launch pad to an exciting future.

2

What about Values?

Should the school curriculum have a section on 'values'? If so, what are the values that ought to be taught? Social media today is abuzz with many opinions on this subject. Whilst there seems to a broad agreement on the principle that values must be taught in school, there is no unanimity on what constitutes these values. For some, it is going back to the Upanishadic traditions; for others, it is to respond to the demands made by a rapidly changing world, and the debate goes on. It often gets very heated and finding a middle ground seems to be a very daunting task.

To my mind, as a teacher, the matter of a 'values curriculum' (if one may call it that), is a very simple one. It is all about producing a good citizen—one who believes in the fundamental ethics of honesty, integrity, respect and empathy for fellow human beings, irrespective of artificial constructs such as race, colour, religion, caste or gender. The one acid test for a value in my opinion is to ask oneself: 'Will it make the world a better and happier place for most?'

Having said that, how does one teach values in school? In our childhood days, we had a subject called 'Moral Science'. How anyone could be so naïve as to believe that parroting the goody-goody lessons in that textbook would help us evolve into noble human beings, beggars belief.

Similarly, of late, there have been attempts to introduce 'Value Education' as a subject. Politicians never tire of exhorting schools to teach values (though heaven knows with what moral authority they do so). The great danger with this exercise is that apart from it being a futile exercise like its predecessor, Moral Science, it can easily degenerate into an attempt at ideological brainwashing.

One incident from my own schooldays will remain forever etched in my memory. Mr Sayeed was our English teacher and Scoutmaster. He was the quintessential schoolmaster and an embodiment of all the virtues we so badly lack these days—honesty, integrity and dedication. The school had once organized a fete to raise money for the Boy Scouts troop. One of the great attractions was a horse ride, courtesy two horses and their 'sowars' (riders) borrowed from the local mounted police.

At some point of the proceedings, one of the horses took fright and bolted across the field. Mr Sayeed happened to be walking across the other end. Completely ignoring the frightened screams around him, he planted himself firmly in the path of the galloping horse with his arms raised to the sky. The petrified animal came to a halt on its haunches, agonizing inches away from our teacher. Mr Sayeed then calmly grasped its bridle and, whispering soothing endearments into the panicked animal's ears, led it away to a quiet spot to allow it to graze and recover from the trauma.

It was an act of personal courage and compassion which etched itself on my mind (especially when I think of how the police horse, Shaktiman, was treated![1]). Here was my teacher practising what he preached in the classroom. It taught me a massive lesson, which I passionately believe in as an educator—*values cannot be taught, they must be walked.*

Of course, today we have the SUPW (Socially Useful Productive Work) programmes in our curriculum. But as any honest teacher will tell you, by and large, the programme has rapidly degenerated into a fake exercise, where students are happy with achieving the minimum attendance requirement and the passing grade, and teachers are happy to oblige.

And yet, the need to add, if one may call it that, a 'moral backbone' to our education system is self-evident. For a long time, the widespread corruption in our country was sought to be explained by the existence of poverty. Others sought an explanation in the prevalence of bureaucracy and red tape. How, then, do we explain the dishonesty and greed that we see in the so-called 'top echelons' of our society, who are affected neither by poverty nor bureaucracy? An article[2] in *The Times of India* (TOI) highlighted the following:

> A survey conducted by the consultancy EY shows how inconsistency in encouraging ethical standards by corporates has led to employees justifying unethical behavior at the workplace. 58 per cent or three in every

---

[1]Shaktiman was injured during a protest march in March 2016 in Dehradun. The police horse died a month later.

[2]Ayyar, Ranjani, '3 of 5 professionals willing to work in cos involved in corruption cases', *The Times of India*, 15 June 2017; https://timesofindia.indiatimes.com/business/india-business/3-of-5-professionals-willing-to-work-in-cos-involved-in-corruption-cases/articleshow/59150267.cms

five of Indian professionals surveyed, were willing to work in an organization involved in major bribery or fraud cases, EY's Asia-Pacific Fraud Survey 2017 found.

Surely, the problem is a deep-rooted one. And to my mind, there is an intrinsic connection with what happens in schools, where teachers are so preoccupied with finishing syllabi or churning out 'hundred percenters' that there is no time for reflection on any kind of values. On the contrary, schools have been known to encourage their students to cheat on the playfield (fudging of dates of birth being widespread) and in the examination hall because advertising their sporting success and '100 per cent board exam result' is of vital importance, from many points of view—not least of all, that of the principal who is under great pressure from the management. And examination boards, too, often, turn a blind eye to all the skullduggery that goes on. Ask anyone familiar with the quality of invigilation at the examination centres and you will know what the sad truth is. Bihar hits the headlines all the time, but it is only the symptom of a nationwide disease.

I once had to suffer the mortification of reporting one of the students from my own school for the use of unfair means. Since the centre Superintendent seemed reluctant to take action, I ended up calling the Chairperson of the Examination Board, whom I happened to know rather well, to report the matter. I was strongly advised to drop the whole thing in view of the possible legal ramifications, and the Board's reluctance to go down that road, in view of the likely publicity fallout.

So where do we go from here, if we are indeed to teach those universal values that I spoke of earlier? The answer, perhaps, lies in attempting to create a culture in school where *everyone*, from management downwards, 'walks the talk'. The usual response from the sceptics will be, 'How on earth can you expect everyone in the school to think this way?' The answer is—you cannot, but there is nothing to stop you from trying. And heaven knows, in the making of that effort, if a school is able to convince even a few of its community of the validity of these values, a small step will have been taken in the right direction.

Let me illustrate this with a few examples. One of the grey areas in a school, especially in one that is highly sought-after, is the admission process. Whispers abound in the marketplace about who should be paid what in order to secure admission. One of the first things that helps bolster a school's credibility is an absolutely transparent admission process. In the schools that I headed, I was very fortunate that I had the total backing of the Board of Governors on this issue. I did, however, persuade the Board to allot a quota for students with learning disabilities, which, too, carried total transparency.

Given the culture of our country, however, there will always be those who will try and buck the system. One incident that I recall vividly occurred in a well-known residential school that I was heading. The school itself happened to be a centre for its entrance examination (there were centres all over the country and abroad). On one such occasion on the day the examination was being conducted, I returned home in the evening to find a rather gaudily packaged gift lying on the centre table. My younger daughter (who was all of four years of age at the time), explained to me that a very 'nice uncle' had left this for me. I opened the packet to find a hefty gold chain inside!

The uncle had very thoughtfully left his visiting card behind. I quickly called the number to discover that this was a father who had brought his daughter for the entrance examination, and now was on his way back to his hometown, which was about six hundred kilometres away. I politely informed the gentleman that I was about to tear up his daughter's answer sheet and flush it down the toilet. The man was reduced to a blabbering mess. He pleaded with me to desist from doing any such thing and assured me that he was turning his vehicle around and driving back straight away.

The man was as good as his word and arrived at my doorstep in the early hours of the morning. In his hands he carried a rather large stick, and he implored me to beat him with it, but to not hurt his daughter's chances of admission! His defence was, 'I do this almost every day whilst conducting business. How was I to know that it would be different here?' As it turned out later, the little girl topped the entrance examination, and I had the opportunity to thoroughly berate the father for having such a low opinion of his own daughter's abilities.

When incidents like this happen in a school environment, they become public knowledge rather quickly. And this, in a way, 'sets the tone' for the institution. Once the children have got the cue, it is amazing where they can carry the ball.

There was this wonderful thing that happened at one of the schools I headed. One of the students was caught on repeated occasions indulging in substance abuse. The fact that he was from an underprivileged background and was on a scholarship, made matters worse. The disciplinary committee warned him on several occasions and administered strictures as well, but to no avail.

Finally, when it seemed that the writing was on the wall and he would have to part ways with the school, a group of students approached me, saying that they would undertake personal responsibility to keep their schoolmate on the straight and narrow. They begged for six months' time to see the experiment through. And they were as good as their word. They formed a phalanx around their friend, and did not let him out of their sight even for a minute. Whenever temptation beckoned, they were around to help, and in some cases even sought the help of their teachers. Slowly but surely, the young man turned around and graduated with flying colours, both in the classroom and on the playing field!

Emboldened by this success, the student body took on a crusade against substance abuse. They made a rather moving feature film on the subject, wrote and performed street theatre all over the city and collaborated with a non-governmental organization (NGO) to send those willing for rehabilitation. As the problem of substance abuse has become a huge one, it will merit a little more discussion subsequently.

On yet another occasion, the students of another school that I was heading at the time, persuaded all the schools in the district to join them in a peaceful march to protest the killing, by religious bigots, of the Australian missionary Graham Staines and his sons. The sons, incidentally, had studied in one of the neighbouring schools in the district and many of my students felt that a show of solidarity and protest was required. It is quite amazing what children can do, once the culture of the school encourages them to move in that direction.

It then becomes vital for the school to sustain this culture. And this is where the role of the principal and at least a core team of teachers becomes crucial. They must keep reinforcing this culture at all levels by constantly encouraging the students to take the initiative. It is vital for all of us as teachers to remind ourselves that whilst it is important to educate the mind, it is equally, if not more, important, to 'educate' the heart and the soul. And as the above examples show, students are only too happy to seize the opportunity.

Much research is being done these days on the business of 'discrimination' in schools. Children do discriminate, on the basis of ethnicity, colour, religion and ability, amongst others. But this is all 'learnt' behaviour, based on what they have picked up from adults. Sadly, most schools do not address this issue, either because it is easier to appear to 'not notice', or because they lack the resources to do so, or worse still, because teachers subscribe to these prejudices themselves.

It all begins with teachers 'branding' some students in their class as 'stupid' or 'slow'. Children pick up on these cues very easily, and one pernicious practice leads to another. And then we have the phenomenon of schools going gaga over their board exam 'toppers', and completely ignoring those who tried, but for reasons beyond their control could not make the cut. Discrimination becomes hard-wired into the system.

In a very disturbing article[3] in the TOI, Nazia Erum writes:

> As many as 80% of Muslim children I spoke to had experienced some form of religious bullying, from as

---

[3]Erum, Nazia, 'Divide and school policy ghettoising Muslim kids', *The Times of India*, 7 January 2018; https://timesofindia.indiatimes.com/home/sunday-times/all-that-matters/divide-and-school-policy-ghettoising-muslim-kids/articleshow/62395438.cms

young as six. The bullies were almost certainly taking their cues from their parents and what they picked up at home. But what was more worrying was that some schools are also unconsciously creating religious divides.

Erum's research shows that across North India schools that have thirty or more Muslim students bunch them together in one class. This, as one can imagine, will have a devastating impact on not only how the Muslim children grow up and what world view they acquire, but also on their peers amongst the other communities.

Teachers often complain that the syllabus load is too heavy for them to do anything else. This is because they view classroom teaching and value education as two distinct entities. The fact is that they are not. After all, what does it take to weave into your lesson advice for your students to respect each other, not to cheat, to be polite to all, to be punctual, to look after their immediate surroundings and so on? And, indeed, to keep reminding them of these on every occasion, inside and outside the classroom? These basic values should be part of the DNA of a school, in the very air that everyone breathes. It does not take separate teaching time or a structured curriculum. It should be who we are. When I hear about young, educated people, stalking, raping or driving with scant respect for the lives of others, I often wonder, if we teachers had carried out a crusade on sensitizing our wards to these issues, would we be in the sorry state that we are in today?

For those looking at the syllabus structure in order to teach values, what better opportunity than the environment? Unfortunately, what we have done with this wonderful opportunity, is to reduce it to an 'examination subject'; encouraged a host of fly-by-night publishers to produce, almost overnight, 'textbooks' on it; and compelled schools that have no trained faculty to deliver the goods by asking the most incompetent science teacher to teach this subject.

And yet, if schools were to seriously try and inculcate a genuine love for the environment, so many values such as caring, sharing, empathy and kindness would automatically fall into place! City schools may still have an excuse (though if tackled imaginatively, love for the environment can be taught anywhere), but what about schools in an area in the lap of nature like Dehradun? How many of the hundreds of schools here encourage birding, identifying trees and plants or even visiting Rajaji National Park—a sanctum of biodiversity and just a stone's throw from the city? A handful, perhaps.

The recent disturbing trend amongst schools is to try and make the prospectus look attractive and outsource 'excursions' to travel companies. The last thing on the mind of these agents is to encourage a love for nature. On the other hand, the attempt is to provide five-star facilities to the clients by way of food, travel and stay, with TV and video games thrown in for good measure. Whilst I fully appreciate that TV, video games and the like are here to stay, I do feel that there is an appropriate time and place for everything, and that by not drawing boundaries, we are seriously impairing the development of a very vital dimension of our children's lives.

And if one wants to give value education a simple structure, it is not at all difficult. I used to ask the students to write a short five-minute play for morning assembly every Monday that would illustrate the spirit of any one value which they felt was important. It was amazing what they could imagine, put into a script, and then act out in front of the entire school.

Similarly, we wrote and performed street theatre all over the city on subjects such as substance abuse, wife beating, dowry and what-have-you. A whole number of life skills were learnt in the process, in addition to deepening their understanding of good citizenship. An 'each one teach one' programme was put in place, whereby each senior student took on the responsibility of teaching the child of one of the support staff after their school hours. It was heart-warming to see the kind of bonding that developed as a result.

The lessons students learn from these opportunities often stay with them for life. The head boy of a residential school that I once headed, spearheaded a campaign to raise a corpus from which the medical expenses of the support staff of the school could be met. (This was in an era when medical insurance was hugely unaffordable.) Almost two decades later, when we met, he asked me what my greatest worry in retirement was. 'My medical expenses,' I replied, 'since no medical insurance is prepared to cover me on account of the multiplicity of problems I suffer from.'

A little over a year later, I received a call from this young man. 'I believe I have cracked your problem,' he said. 'I have persuaded a bunch of my friends from our schooldays to join me in raising a rather large corpus to cover the needs of all the teachers who taught us and do not have access to medical insurance.' No accolades, no recognition that anyone could offer could equal the joy and fulfillment I felt when I heard those words!

A very emotive, value-laden subject that is of great concern these days is one relating to gender sensitivity and, indeed, gender violence. Given the kinds of incidents that seem to be on the rise these days and amongst the so-called 'educated youth', it is obvious that we are missing something in the way we are imparting education.

There was a great deal of debate recently on the subject of 'sex-education'. It did generate a lot of noise with large numbers coming down in favour and also against. Unfortunately, in the ensuing din, the real issue was obfuscated. After all, what are we educating our children for? Amongst other things, I assume it is to learn to live with and respect each other, irrespective of gender or sexual orientation. After all, the real world is co-ed, and with people of different sexual preferences, is it not?

Children who are perceived to be 'gay' are very often given a torrid time of it by their peers. There is a great need for sensitization in this area as, indeed, there is on the issue of transgender people and how important it is to respect them. These issues are buried largely because we adults have not been able to overcome our own dark prejudices. And what with women increasingly challenging the assumptions of a patriarchal society, and pushing the frontiers of their own achievements, is it not necessary to re-examine the road map in this area?

Schools, however, have been, largely, very disappointing in their response. How many schools have taken it upon themselves to sensitize faculty on this matter? The all-too-familiar scenario when a young girl in the classroom wishes to be 'excused' and the male teacher refuses, suspecting that he is being taken for a ride, whilst the rest of the class breaks into knowing smiles and uneasy titters, is not just a stereotype.

It happens every day.

I was once heading a prestigious boys' boarding school, which happened to have its 'sister' school right next door. It seemed to me that, in the circumstances, the most natural (and sensible) thing to do was to synergize the efforts of both schools by having classes and activities together, since the boarding facilities were safely separated anyway. My suggestion to this effect was received with the horrified response, 'All that will happen is that the boys and girls will distract each other!' If this is the response in our educated, elite schools, one shudders to think of what happens with our less 'enlightened' counterparts.

Some schools try and sidestep the problem by hiring resource persons to deliver 'sex education' classes. But a PowerPoint presentation, accompanied, perhaps, by a lot of jargon, can never be a substitute for a kindly teacher putting his/her arms around the shoulders of a troubled child and encouraging a discussion, as it were, on the birds and bees. Some schools have 'counsellors', but there is much to be done for genuine counselling in this country.

Ideally, schools will have to invest both time and money to train teachers to guide children through this minefield—with sympathy, understanding, confidentiality—and drive home the fundamental value of respecting each other. And teachers, if they are to reach out to students, will have to rid themselves of their own prejudices and inhibitions. The role of parents in dealing with this tricky issue is a vital one and merits discussion in another chapter.

It is impossible, in any discussion of this nature, to get away from the issue of religion. Should there be religious instruction in schools? If so, what should be the curriculum?

At schools, as indeed in most institutions, most auspicious events are preceded by a 'puja'. Is that appropriate? These are tricky questions to which there are no easy answers.

Swami Agnivesh, in an article[4] in *The Indian Express*, perhaps provides the best way forward when he says, 'Religion turns human beings towards God, so that they are led out of narrow-mindedness. Therefore, any religion which advocates divisive agendas is an insult to God and human beings.'

The Swami goes on to propose the following priorities: 'First, the indoctrination of children from birth onwards regarding a single faith, so that their freedom of choice is virtually abolished, should stop. Second, children, through education, must be familiarized with world religions, so that they can make informed choices. Third, every attempt must be made to promote a critical mind in children... Religions, as agents of liberation, must promote free enquiry.'

To the Swami's list, I would like to add another suggestion: Atheism should also be presented as a possible choice to children, indeed with all its pros and cons.

There is also a great deal of debate these days about 'spirituality' and 'religion'. Not being an accomplished theologian, all I can say is that whereas religion attaches itself to a core set of beliefs, spirituality is a state where an individual perhaps acknowledges the presence of a greater being than himself, but does not attach that belief to any core dogma, or indeed the feeling that his belief system is superior to that

---

[4] Agnivesh, Swami, 'Real Freedom of Religion', *The Indian Express*, 9 June 2017; https://indianexpress.com/article/opinion/columns/real-freedom-of-religion-4695420/

of anyone else. This helps eliminate conflict.

Schools can certainly encourage spirituality. Just the simple expedient of a daily assembly, where everyone sits in silence for a short while, reflects on the day ahead and, perhaps, hears some non-denominational prayer or hymn, can do a lot towards helping young minds in this direction.

Just as, in the words of the Swami, 'The worst disservice religions do is that by promoting orthodoxy, they kill free thinking, innovation, and initiative which despoils our potential,' so too, an education system that entraps the mind, forces it to think in narrow compartments, discourages an empathetic and open mind that respects and seeks to learn from others who are different, is bound to catapult our society back into an era of darkness and ignorance.

It is worthwhile to remind ourselves of the famous appeal made to teachers by a school principal who survived the Nazi camps. He wrote:

> I am a survivor of a concentration camp. My eyes saw what no person should witness. Gas chambers built by learned engineers. Children poisoned by educated physicians. Infants killed by trained nurses. Women and babies shot and killed by high school and college graduates. So, I am suspicious of education. My request is, help your students to be human. Your efforts must never produce learned monsters, skilled psychopaths, or educated maniacs. Reading, writing, and spelling and history and arithmetic are only important if they serve to make our students more human.

From being obsessed with producing 'toppers', schools will

have to, in the jargon, make 'a paradigm shift' in their priorities. Yes, the nation needs its doctors, lawyers, engineers and businessmen. But more importantly, we need to unleash a generation that will go forth, in the words of the prayer: '…as weapons polished and keen/wherewith they may fight the battle of righteousness and truth/vanquishing error, oppression and wrong.'

3

The Scourge of Bullying

Bullying is an evil that has affected children and schools all over the world. Every teacher would have encountered it in some form or the other. There are several factors, which, in my opinion, aid and abet this evil in our society. The fact that we have a caste system that for all purposes institutionalizes bullying; that in many of our own homes it is an accepted practice to bully servants; that the children of the affluent and privileged are brought up to believe that they can get away with veritable murder, the fact that many indeed do and all pleas for justice are drowned out—all these mould the environment that we bring up our children in, and they can, and do, have an impact on young, impressionable minds.

During the course of my career, I have seen bullying in all forms—from the most blatant acts of older boys beating the life out of their younger compatriots, to the slightly more 'sophisticated' technique of getting younger boys to run errands for them (and all through the night at times), to girls carrying out the most subtle forms of mental torture against a hapless victim.

The problem tends to be a little worse in boarding schools than in day schools, purely because boarders live with each other in communal surroundings for the greater part of the year. Boarding schools also tend to be very hierarchical in nature with the added element of certain 'traditions' such as bullying becoming institutionalized.

This, in turn, means that anyone who dares to challenge the pecking order, usually comes a cropper. This is why there is a dominant tendency in most boarding schools to follow a 'herd mentality', and it takes an unusually brave person to break with the 'herd'. This trait, I am afraid, persists, in some cases, well into adult life, as I have seen middle-aged alumni club together and close ranks against one of their group who they perceive as 'different' and threaten their 'unity' (which in most cases revolves around a uniformity in thinking). And in my experience, it is the brave soul who dares to be different, who actually ends up being a leader in later life.

To return, however, to bullying. One of the most disturbing cases I have ever come across was that of a Class IX student in a well-known boarding school that I was heading. As a Class IX student, he, like the others in his class, was considered to be 'the lowest of the low' in the pecking order of the senior school which consisted of Classes IX–XII. The sole justification for the existence of Class IX students (as codified in the school traditions) was to serve the senior-most class. In fact, each of the seniors had a special 'slave' attached to him to run all his errands and do his chores. Failure to perform these duties in line with the expectation of the 'master' could attract brutal reprisal, including a sound thrashing with hockey sticks, or even branding with an electric iron!

It so happened that on one occasion, a particularly bad case of bullying was reported to me, surreptitiously, of course. As soon as I started taking action, word went around that this particular Class IX student had 'snitched'.

Of course he was beaten. But much worse was to follow. The seniors, and his own peers, organized a campaign to ostracize the hapless victim. He was boycotted at meals, in the classroom, on the sports field and in the dormitory. Late at night, his bed would be shifted to the toilet. All the counselling, pleading and talking to the students failed to break the impasse. The poor lad could not take it any more and fell seriously ill. As a matter of fact, the doctors diagnosed a clot in the brain, and he had to be shifted to Delhi for treatment.

I considered it a personal failure and advised the parents to withdraw the boy from the school. But neither the boy, nor his parents would hear of this. As soon as the young man recovered, he was back. This was the biggest kick in the teeth for the bullies, though I daresay I had my heart in my mouth through this entire 'experiment'.

The young man went on to excel himself at school, and about a year back called me proudly from the US to announce that he had just launched his own start-up. Not all stories, however, have such happy endings, and I have known more than my fair share of sad ones.

The fact is that incidents of this nature probably occur on almost a daily basis in schools across the country. The public conscience is, however, stirred only when the media bombards us with these tragic stories and organizes panel discussions on television with the 'experts'. So what is the answer, if any?

Any attempt to answer this question must first make a distinction between 'bullying' and 'ragging'. Incidents of the nature I have described are tantamount to bullying. This is the kind of sadistic behaviour displayed by a senior (or a group of seniors) to give sanctity to the pecking order, particularly in the older boarding schools. Over a period of time, these sadistic practices become part of the hallowed traditions of the school.

Bullying in day schools tends to be different. In a day school, it is less of a cultural thing and more of an individual or gang-related phenomenon—either a powerful individual attracts the support of a gang of admirers, who then prey upon the weaker ones, or there is a proliferation of gangs who fight each other over a host of issues (in a co-ed school, often for the attention of the girls).

It may seem from the above that bullying is purely a male phenomenon. Nothing could be further from the truth. Girls also bully, though they do not usually get involved in physical violence. Nonetheless, their bullying is just as vicious and hurtful. It is subtle, often psychological—with taunts, social boycotts involved—and in the end, just as damaging.

Ragging is different—it is a sort of initiation rite, practised in colleges. It was fairly prevalent in the US where it went under the name of 'hazing'. It drew its inspiration mainly from the harsh practices in the military academies, meant to toughen up would-be officers.

These rites of initiation, which can range from the ludicrous to the barbaric, usually do not last very long, and are terminated after a welcoming ceremony which is held a few weeks into the new term. The 'freshers' are then regarded as regular members of the college fraternity. Of course, those few weeks often take a gruesome toll.

In TV debates on the subject, many experts claim that bullies are normally from maladjusted backgrounds and have probably suffered some deep emotional scarring in early childhood. Whilst that may be true in some cases, my experience has been that most bullies in India have grown up in an environment of entitlement and privilege and consider it their natural right to lord it over others.

As I have pointed out earlier, bullying is endemic to our culture. The caste system, the entitlement of those born to privilege and wealth, all encourage bullying.

How many times have principals faced the wrath of rich and privileged parents who take up cudgels for their child who has openly flouted school rules? I once had to deal with a group of parents whose sons had deliberately tried to engineer a strike-like situation in the school, despite all our efforts at counselling. When I suspended the students, the parents took me to court! It was heartening to see that the court not only upheld my decision, but also delivered a severe admonishment to the parents.

But there are no winners in this sort of a situation. It is 'lose-lose' all around. Children are quick to pick up these cues from their parents, and we see the effects every day. One of the lines most heard by our policemen is, '*Jante ho mera baap kaun hai*? (Do you know who my father is?)' At a very basic level, what happened to Jessica Lal[5] was an act of bullying. We are well-behaved in foreign countries only because our bullying tactics do not work there.

Parents must seriously evaluate their responsibility in this matter. What kind of role models are they at home? How do

---

[5] In 1999, Jessica Lal was shot dead by a man when she refused to serve him a drink in a Delhi restaurant.

they deal with their employees? How many times do we see families dining out in style, when the poor ayah, who has been brought along as a babysitter, sits forlornly in the foyer? All these actions create the culture of a society. What is the reaction of parents when their child does something wrong? More often than not, it is of complete denial, if not outright aggression.

The biggest challenge for schools is to provide an atmosphere that is free of fear. For this, it is critical to have a clear-cut disciplinary code in which all offenders, irrespective of status or family, are dealt with in equal measure. There will be times when harsh decisions will have to be taken. And there will be an inevitable backlash in the form of pressure—political, bureaucratic and others—but the institution must stand firm.

I myself have had to resist pressure from an organization no less than the Prime Minister's Office (PMO), but I stood my ground successfully, which is also a tribute to the sagacity of the then PMO. It has been my experience that if the decision is a fair one, arrived at by consensus, is in the interests of the institution and is consistently followed in all cases, it is not too difficult to resist pressures.

The persecuted must be encouraged to speak out. For this it is important that the staff be trained to look out for the first signs—an apathetic attitude, dropping grades and sullenness are some of the common ones. It is then important that every teacher makes it his/her business to reach out and win the trust of the victim. It helps to have trained counsellors who can help teachers in this process. Colleagues can also help each other out. The child concerned must have total faith in the fact that they will not, in any way, suffer, should the matter be exposed.

This is not an easy battle, and it often takes years of sustained effort to develop such a culture. Not only the principal, but the entire faculty must speak in one voice—to the bullies as well as the bullied. It has to be a veritable crusade. Constant vigilance is another pillar of this crusade. No institution can afford to let its guard down in the mistaken belief that it has rooted out this evil, because this is a pernicious practice and has a way of creeping back.

With the advent of cyberbullying, yet another dimension has been added to this scourge. Not having any experience, or indeed expertise, in this matter, I am not in a position to offer any solutions, other than those that common sense and my experience as an educator tell me. Cyberbullying being a relatively new phenomenon, society is still trying to get to grips with its implications. It seems to me that schools will have to tackle this problem at various levels.

The first of these is, of course, the 'technical' level. Keeping in mind that students will always be one step ahead of their teachers in this respect, schools will necessarily have to fall back on the help of experts to build as many safeguards as possible in this domain.

Equally, if not more importantly, it is imperative to engage the entire school community (teachers, parents, management, counsellors, students, alumni) in an ongoing discussion on the subject. The aim would be to sensitize everybody to the grave dangers posed by this threat, encourage those victimized to feel supported and actively seek support and create an environment where perpetrators, or potential perpetrators, are positively discouraged from continuing with this evil practice.

Unlike in the case of physical bullying, it is more often than not very difficult to identify cyberbullies, and this makes the task unimaginably more difficult. This is why the entire school community must support each other in this battle.

Bullying can often be the product of boredom—the pursuit of an unchallenged mind. Institutions that provide a joyful learning experience, both in the classroom and outside it, and constantly challenge their students intellectually and in physical activity, are more likely to avoid this curse.

Engagement in learning experiences where the focus shifts from 'I' to 'we'— for instance, in community projects, theatre, adventure activities—is a great antidote to this blight. Schools today, unfortunately, have become so obsessed with marks and tuitions, with sending as large a contingent to the IITs as possible, that the real spirit of education has been seriously compromised.

Bullying is not going to be eradicated by a Supreme Court order or Presidential ordinance. It will require the active cooperation and engagement of all sections of civil society, if this scourge is to be eradicated.

4

The Leadership and Management of Schools

To most people, the running of a school seems a relatively easy business. This is a perception fostered by the fact, that almost all of us have attended school at some point of our lives and, therefore, feel that the journey through school gives us some very enabling insights into its running. Principals, will, therefore, never be short of all and sundry offering them advice on how to go about their business. The truth, however, is that the running of a school is a very complex business, and in this day and age, fraught with all kinds of pressures and pitfalls. It can often turn out to be a very challenging task.

To begin with, let us look at what is usually referred to as the 'Management' of the school. In the case of most private schools, this actually refers to the owner, or owners, of the school. This ownership is at most times, vested in a rather extended family. Some owners do go to the trouble of creating a 'Board of Advisers' to give a fig leaf of respectability to the enterprise. However, in most cases, all powers are vested with the owner and his/her family. This structure creates its own ecosystem, where, by and large, the driving motive is the profitability of the enterprise. And this brings in its wake, constant interference in the day-to-day running of the school.

Then there are the venerable 'Public Schools'—the legacy of our colonial past and our answer to the Etons and Harrows of the world. These are usually run by a Society or Trust, and all the powers rest with a Board of Governors. With rare exceptions, most of these Boards have little or no understanding of the real issues that touch a school's life. The driving force here is usually the ability of the school to massage the egos of the Board.

I once took over a well-known public school, to discover that the Vice-Principal in situ was an old (public) school friend of the Chairman. Neither of them had any background in education, and one of the conditions of employment of the Vice-Principal was that he had the right to go off for golf each afternoon, and over the weekends! And that was not all. Some of the honourable members turned up for meetings perhaps once in two years, and there were two who faithfully slept through every meeting they attended! If this was indeed the state in a so-called 'premier school', the mind boggles at what might be happening in the 'lesser' places.

The government schools have their own ecosystems, with all the trappings of bureaucratic indifference and interference, and all the certainties and uncertainties that characterize 'sarkari' institutions. The great tragedy of our education system is that in most cases, the levers of control are vested with people who have very little idea of education—just as the tragedy of sport in this country is that control is vested in non-sportspersons.

The person reporting to the management (whatever shape that entity assumes) is the principal. S/he is usually a 'teacher on promotion' (at least when they assume that position for the first time), with no training for the job. I have often wondered whether the army would promote someone with no specific training as say, a Brigade Commander, or indeed a corporate house, an untrained executive as the Head of a division? It happens only in our schools!

The principal's relationship with the management is a very delicate one. Increasingly, and regrettably, of late, most managements prefer to have a 'manager' rather than a 'leader' as the Head of the institution. This means that as long as the principal does the management's bidding, does not rock the boat and remains 'politically correct', everyone lives happily ever after. How one wrests back that 'leadership space', is something that I will revert to later, and in my opinion, is the bedrock of leadership in a school.

If the principal has the Scylla of the management on the one hand, s/he has the Charybdis of a host of constituencies on the other. These are the students, the faculty, the parents, the local community and, in some cases, the alumni. (The last, incidentally, are more powerful in the older residential schools than they are in the day schools, and can be the institution's biggest strength or indeed its Achilles heel.)

The principal has to skillfully negotiate the demands and expectations of all these constituencies. I remember heading a school in Kolkata that was managed by twenty 'trustees', each of whom had put in an equal amount of money into the enterprise. I recall numerous occasions when I took a decision (particularly during admissions), and one of the trustees would call to say what an excellent decision that had been. The next minute, another trustee would call and scream at me to reverse that decision—the accompanying admonishment being, 'Do you think X has paid more than I have?' And this is why I say that this is not a job for the faint-hearted!

So what does 'leadership' imply in these circumstances? Not having a degree in management or even attended one of the popular leadership courses that seem to be on offer these days (or read one of the numerous books that promise to teach you leadership in ten easy lessons!), I can only offer insights based on my own experience, which have worked (or not worked, depending on one's perspective) for me in various situations.

The most critical brick that goes into the making of leadership (especially for a school Head) is a clear picture of what they expect the school to be. What, for instance, is the young person who is going to graduate from that institution, going to stand for? What are the skill sets a young person will possess, after having finished from that institution? Many would call this a 'vision'. I hesitate to do so, as the term has become part of business management jargon. Yet, it is imperative. And once this vision is clear and decided (it is best decided by extensive consultation with all stakeholders, i.e. management, faculty, students, parents, alumni), everything that the Head does must be in consonance with this bigger picture. This approach obviously has its dangers, as people are quick to forget what they have signed up for when it does not suit their interests, but it is vital if the institution has to stand for something, and sometimes even survive.

It also means that a good Head must have great moral courage because s/he will be constantly challenged on that front. And the challenges can come from the most unexpected quarters.

At one of the residential schools that I headed, within a year of having taken over, I was confronted with a strike of the support staff union. This, despite the fact that I had been in constant touch with them and the school board had been scrupulously fair in dealing with them. To cut a long story short, I had to suspend three of the leaders, who also happened to be the leaders of the state union. The matter, therefore, became a political hot potato. My house was besieged, for almost a month, by hundreds of striking employees, along with their colleagues from other unions, and their families. Bricks were hurled through my windows and, to my great embarrassment, a personal security officer had to be hired to accompany me everywhere! Politicians, cutting across party lines, threatened me with dire consequences.

The Board of Governors of the school, in their wisdom, left me to take whatever decision I felt fit under the circumstances, with the proviso that whatever the outcome, the accountability was totally mine. It was truly a double-edged sword that I had been handed!

Some things were very clear to me. The simplest option would be to reinstate the three suspended employees. The strike would be called off, the siege would be lifted and life would go back to normal.

I could always justify this decision on the grounds of the 'general good' of the entire school community. But could I justify this decision to myself? Would I ever be able to run the school in a free and independent manner?

And, more importantly, if the union got away with these tactics, what would prevent all the other schools around from falling like ninepins to this onslaught? It is a different matter that not even one Head of school called me during this entire crisis, to either enquire about our welfare or offer help. They did, however, congratulate me once the strike was called off, and thank me profusely for taking a stand and sparing them a similar fate!

The strike was eventually called off, without the three suspended employees being reinstated, the union was dissolved (and remains so) and mechanisms were created for the redressal of all employee issues. And I am proud to say that one of the warmest send-offs I got when I left the school was from the support staff.

The strike taught me that it is always possible to use a crisis to gain some very positive results. First of all, it sent a clear message to the entire community that the school would not be cowed down by threats or blackmail—an essential step in wresting back the 'leadership space' alluded to earlier. I learnt some very useful lessons in media management. Media—electronic and print—was at our doorstep every day. I not only welcomed them, but also made it a point to keep them honestly briefed on the situation. Consequently, a very important partner in moulding public opinion was on the school's side.

Equally importantly, the strike fostered a great deal of camaraderie within the school community. After all, for almost a month, it was the faculty and students who together kept this boarding school running.

Given the complexity of this exercise, this was no easy feat. Throughout the crisis, I made it a point to consult with senior faculty on every step that we took. The students, too, were kept in the loop (apart from the fact that they actually ran the school), and I made it a point to emphasize to them that the support staff had been misled, that some of their families had served the school for generations and that when they returned to their duties, they were to be treated with the respect and affection that they deserved.

A very interesting aspect of the strike was that during the entire course of this event, not one member of the Board ever visited the school. Knowing that they were not very keen to do so anyway, I too discouraged them. This gave me the space to work with my colleagues, devise our strategies and take our decisions. This was a bit of a calculated risk—if things turned out right, we would come out of it all appearing to be in total command; but, if things went wrong, we could not shift the blame. The gamble paid off. Principals do get opportunities to reclaim leadership space, but they must have the courage to run the gauntlet.

And this brings me to another great challenge for leaders— team building. It is all very well to have a vision in place—but what use is that vision, if those responsible on the ground for its implementation are not on board?

The school I had taken over was a very fractured community. The faculty members were at loggerheads with each other, and it was so bad that on one occasion two of the male teachers nearly got into a fist fight in front of the students! Many of the old guard were very sceptical about a new principal. The parents had lost faith in the school because of the prevailing indiscipline, worsened by a problem of widespread substance abuse. This, in turn, led to disastrous academic results. The students themselves, like all adolescents, were happy to take advantage of this divided community, and the resulting chaos was frightening.

The strike, however, helped this fractured community close ranks, and its successful closure brought about a great sense of confidence in the entire school community. They could now take on any challenge thrown at them!

Sensing this new spirit, I took full advantage to stretch them to the limit and build a team in the process. A disciplinary committee was created with a majority of students on it, a senior management committee was installed with senior faculty being made responsible for collective decision-making on critical issues, a staff forum was created where interpersonal differences amongst faculty were sorted out with the help of a senior 'ombudsman' (duly elected), study groups were formed within the faculty to discuss and improve curriculum, sport was given pride of place in the school's scheme of things—'We were good enough to take on an entire union. Surely, we are good enough to build a great school,' was the spirit. Slowly, but surely the vision was being shared.

One of the critical components of this vision was to move away from the traditional 'chalk and talk' pedagogy, to a more progressive teaching-learning programme, which would be more interactive and enquiry based, and foster genuine learning, rather than rote and repeat.

This is a huge challenge for principals, as there is no pool of trained teachers available as there are MBAs in the corporate world. Of course, workshops run by resource persons are a great help. But they are expensive, and profit-conscious managements are reluctant to invest in them. And the sad fact is that most of these 'resource' persons are people who have never taught for a day in their lives and happily tweak some corporate training practices to deliver the goods.

Long-lasting success in this area, in my opinion, can only be achieved if a genuine 'culture of learning' can be created within the school itself, whereby teachers themselves explore and discover new methods and, more importantly, share these with each other. There is a huge amount of material to be found on the Internet, and in literature on the subject, and if teachers can be motivated to form 'study groups' that peruse this material, tweak it to meet the school's needs, and then share it with colleagues, a great deal of learning can be generated. The judicious use of technology is, of course, a huge enabler.

The crux of the matter, however, is the creation of a culture of learning in the school, whereby teachers take on their roles and are prepared to *learn,* both on their own, and with each other. At Welham Boys' School (Dehradun), in particular, such interactive sessions were structured and built into the routine. Moreover, a whole new element was added, when, on occasion, we held these sessions at esoteric locations like national parks and forest rest houses. A lot of fun, camaraderie and bonhomie also became part of the learning package.

Teaching is one profession, which, I am convinced, is worth doing *only* if a teacher wakes up every morning with a sense of joy and excitement at the prospect of the challenges that lie ahead. The challenge of reaching out to young minds, touching young lives, finding new meaning in, and discovering new ways of, being more effective in the classroom and out of it—this is what makes this profession so different, and so worthwhile.

The creation of such a culture is a slow process and needs sustained effort. The whole process begins with what one of my ex-bosses in the corporate world used to say about building a team: 'Nurture their strengths and protect their weaknesses'. In practice, this meant that one had to spot those teachers with a 'spark' and work with them, and through them. It also meant identifying those who were bored and jaded, and offering them a change.

For instance, one of the senior teachers complained that he was bored stiff with his subject. I asked him what he would rather do instead. 'The co-curricular activities interest me,' he said. In no time at all, a post of 'Dean of Activities' was created and a thoroughly rejuvenated faculty member took on the reins with great gusto!

In another case, the students complained that they had a very poor teacher for their subject. I had recruited this person after considerable diligence and was quite taken aback by this feedback. I arranged a series of meetings between the students and their teacher, where a free and informal exchange of views took place. It was a matter of time before the teacher was back on the ball as far as that class was concerned.

Efforts at team building such as these will be rendered meaningless unless teachers are also given the freedom and space to innovate and experiment. One of the principles that worked for me was to 'pick the right person for the job and let him/her get on with it'. Of course there must be supervision and checks, but that is very different from breathing down people's necks and suffocating them. Mistakes will occur, but a good Head will support the person concerned and help 'course-correct'. I distinctly remember my mentor, Shomie Das, calling me over and spending time with me if I had made a mess of some task.

And I am a great believer in the axiom, 'the buck stops

here'. If ever I found my teachers under attack from the parents, the Board, the students or whosoever, the person or persons with the grievance would have to deal with me first and I, in turn, would take it from there. There was at least one occasion when a member of the Board wanted a faculty member sacked (for what I felt were totally unwarranted reasons), and I had to very nearly put my own job on the line for the sake of my colleague. But I would have wanted my own boss to do that for me, if ever the situation arose!

Team building also means that there will be situations, when, for the sake of one's colleagues, a Head will have to cast aside the bureaucratic web that they can often find themselves in, and resort to some unconventional solutions.

In both the boarding schools that I headed, finding funds for staff welfare, especially in cases of medical emergencies, was always a challenge. The loans that employees could avail of were pitiable amounts and barely got anyone past the hospital door. I have already spoken in an earlier chapter of how at both schools we created an 'emergency fund', to which everyone, including the students, contributed voluntarily. The fund was operated by the finance manager, some senior faculty, and student representatives. All applications were carefully vetted, scrutinized and disbursements made. It was also a huge learning experience for the students.

When the funds so raised proved to be insufficient, I had no compunctions about asking wealthy parents, alumni or even my own friends to help out. There was this one time when I was approached for help by one of the teachers (who happened to be my bitterest critic). He was in a state of near panic; it appeared that his daughter had secured admission to one of the prestigious colleges in Coimbatore, and he had only just discovered that a rather hefty donation was required to complete that process. What made the situation more difficult was that the money had to be paid by 4 p.m. on that day, and it was already 10 a.m. when he approached me. Since there was no time to convene a meeting of the committee, I quickly phoned an old college friend who happened to be a successful businessman in that city, and asked him to bail out my colleague. I then had my colleague rushed to the bus station in my car and the admission was achieved. I understand that the young lady is doing quite well in life.

A word of caution, however. No Head should expect any gratitude in return for acts such as these. If one does receive gratitude, it is a bonus. In this particular case, this gentleman, after showering me with profuse thanks and boxes of sweets, went on to stab me in the back. You win some, you lose some… But the rest of the community always gets to know the truth.

In any school, day or boarding, there will always be 'staffroom politics'. A good Head will traverse this minefield only if he is firm in the belief that he is not there to win votes, and that the only motive for any action he takes is the welfare of the school. It is only when powerful outside agencies start manipulating these 'staff groups' (as indeed I discovered much to my detriment in one of the boarding schools I headed) that the pot boils over.

What a team spirit does is also to instil in teachers a sense of pride—something that is badly missing in the profession. When a school represents certain shared values and ideals and if teachers feel that they are the flag-bearers of these values and ideals, and are given the support and respect that they deserve, a certain sense of professional pride is created, which, in turn, positively impacts the teachers' relationship with their students.

Motivating and exciting the students to join in this 'adventure' is perhaps one of the most joyful challenges that come a principal's way. The degree of difficulty varies a lot with every school, depending on its history and past shared experience—in other words, the baggage it carries, or does not carry.

At the first school that I headed, which happened to be 130 years old at the time, the task was formidable. The so-called traditions of the school, most of which were rather colonial and brutal, did not make the job easier. Once again, assembling a core team of the faculty, which, too, believed that change was necessary, was the first step in this battle. Restoring their pride and faith in themselves and the system was the next. Engaging the students in interesting, challenging and varied activities helped in overcoming a great deal of the cynicism and indiscipline that prevailed.

This cynicism was also because the infrastructure was in a shambles, and the students felt a profound sense of neglect. A parallel battle to raise funds had to be waged, and in this I found myself very much on my own. That story would perhaps merit another chapter—but suffice to say that over a period of time significant funding came in and huge improvements were made.

As with the faculty, the idea was to challenge the students to stretch themselves and, at the same time, ensure that they felt cared for. In yet another school that I headed, the simple expedient of handing the students a video camera and asking them to produce a news digest every fortnight on the lines of TV channels, yielded spectacular results. The students, as a matter of fact, went on to produce an award-winning documentary on a local river, entitled, *Who Killed the Rispana*? The young man who directed the film is now a highly successful film-maker! Similar measures were undertaken in almost every area of school life to engage and keep the students involved in creative and meaningful pursuits. A plethora of life skills, which no classroom could ever teach, was acquired as a result.

Such engagement is vital in maintaining the health and discipline of the school. But, at the end of the day, a respect for rules is equally vital. Quite early into my headship, I realized that one way of fostering respect for the rules was to make the students partners in the framing of the rules. Thus, every rule that was introduced was debated and discussed with the representatives of the student body. The understanding was, that once accepted, it went without saying that any violation of the rules would entail acceptance of the penalty that went with this violation. And, in order to judge whether a violation had indeed occurred, and what the nature of the penalty ought to be, a disciplinary committee, in which the students had representation, was instituted.

There has been a great deal of debate about the wisdom of vesting authority in student representatives. I must confess that my experience in this area has been a mixed one. In boarding schools, in particular, I have seen school prefects often degenerate into the worst kind of bullies, no matter how careful one has been in the selection process. I can never forget the advice given to me by an alumnus of the first boarding school I happened to head. 'Pick the biggest bully in the senior-most class and make him head boy. You do not need to worry about discipline after that!' Needless to say that I disregarded the advice, but I still had my bad moments after that, and had to exercise constant vigilance.

That is not to say that there were no positives in this process. I learnt some wonderful lessons from my students. I remember one case where the disciplinary committee had decided to ask a student, who was constantly stealing from the others, to be withdrawn from the school. Subsequently, it was discovered that the student in question came from an extremely humble background, and surrounded by his affluent friends, succumbed repeatedly to temptation. I hurriedly reconvened the committee and asked them if they wished to reconsider their decision.

The students firmly opined that reconsideration was not an option as it would set a bad precedent. Instead, they involved the entire school community in raising funds that would ensure that the young man secured admission in, and could pay the fees for, a good school in his home city. Not only that, they also asked a parent from that city to be a 'mentor' to their friend, and let him be an 'intern' in his own office after school hours! Collaboration, in my opinion, is a key to good leadership.

Working in tandem with parents is something that many principals find to be a daunting task. It is very sad to see, more often than not, a 'them' and 'us' situation between parents and school. This is an unhealthy relationship, and as is the case in a bad marriage, the worst sufferers are the children.

There were a few ground rules that guided me in working with parents. The first one was of complete transparency. Not only at the time of admission, but indeed all through their child's stay in school, I clearly spelt out what the school's expectations were of them and what, in turn, they could expect of the school. I was also equally candid about our successes and failures, as also our problems.

In one of the schools that I took over, there was a serious problem of substance abuse. After much thought, I wrote to all the parents apprising them of the nature and seriousness of the problem. I offered them two alternatives. They could seek another option for their children, and there would be no hard feelings. Or they could join hands with me in fighting this plague. I could only do my best, I told them, but with a problem of this nature there was no guarantee of success. To my surprise, most parents decided to stay on with the school, and together with the students we waged a crusade for a few years and wiped out the scourge. I will touch on this story in some detail later, as I do think it is of critical importance.

There was a sustained attempt to build a genuine partnership. Parents were invited to speak to the students if they had something interesting to relate, or indeed expertise to share. In one school, I actually persuaded the parent body to fund one teacher's study trip to some schools abroad each year. In another, parents offered to invite teachers deputed by the school to spend some time with them as their guests at home for a few days during the vacation. Parents gained some insight into the lives of teachers and vice-versa. The child was the beneficiary of this collaboration. Once again, I will return to this discussion in a subsequent chapter as I do feel that it merits serious consideration.

I am by no means suggesting that all this will totally eliminate any conflict areas between the school and parents.

There will still be parents who will want rules bent to suit them and react very badly when that does not happen. But by and large, if the school is fair and applies the same yardstick to all, irrespective of position or status, parents, albeit grudgingly, see reason.

Alumni, particularly in the older boarding schools, present a different kind of challenge. This is because, unlike their counterparts in a day school, boarding school students develop a greater sense of 'proprietorship' over their alma mater. This then leads not only to a fierce primitive loyalty, but also to a sense of empowerment along the lines of, 'I have a right to decide what is good for the school'. The fact that most of these students come from very privileged backgrounds and are almost conditioned to feel a great sense of entitlement, makes matters worse.

The other factor that comes into play in boarding schools is that they tend to encourage a 'herd' mentality, much more than in day schools. Their hierarchical traditions, embodied in the vast powers that prefects and seniors enjoy, encourage a mentality of 'follow the leaders' (whether they are right or wrong). The ones who dare to question the accepted norms are given a very rough passage indeed. And sadly, this herd mentality sometimes persists in adult life. Principals of these schools, therefore, have to tread very cautiously on this minefield. And it claims many victims, as I can well testify. Yet, in the same breath I will add that the alumni can be the biggest source of strength to a school. For one, their fierce, almost primal, loyalty is there for the school to tap into. Many of them will gladly sacrifice time, money and effort for the sake of their alma mater. Once again, as in the case of 'staffroom politics', much will depend on who the leadership of the alumni is, and what that leadership's agenda is.

At the end of the day, the Head ploughs a lonely furrow. There are so many constituencies out there to balance. But a Head is not appointed to win votes. They must do what in their opinion (an opinion formed after due consultation and research) is best for the school.

The Head must accept that in today's scenario, managements and boards move in mysterious ways and are often driven by agendas that are difficult to fathom. They can also be at times dishonest and cowardly. If this is indeed the nature of our 'educational leadership', then it is not too difficult to explain, perhaps, the abysmal state of affairs in the country as a whole, and the complete lack of any kind of moral leadership. The Head must accept that one day a price may have to be paid. But there is no greater joy, than that of going to bed, knowing that one did the right thing by one's conscience, and by the children entrusted to one's care.

5

Fun and Games

Everyone keeps parroting the adage, 'Childhood is the best time of one's life'. And yet, what are we doing to the childhood of our children? We have reduced it to a soulless grind of school-tuition-examinations. On my way to the airport, one foggy, cold winter morning at about 5 a.m., I came across a group of children on their bicycles. Curious to know why they were up so early, I stopped to ask. They were off to their first round of tuitions! After that, they would go on to school, and immediately after, go on to two or three tuition rounds, before reaching home close to 9.30 p.m. And this is a routine that a disturbingly large number of our children follow. And we expect them to change the world with their joie de vivre and creativity!

Given that in the foreseeable future, this situation is not going to change very much, it is important for schools to provide relief from this soul-destroying grind and give our children something of their childhood back. Of course, imaginative, creative and challenging teaching practices in the classroom go a long way towards relieving the stress and boredom inflicted by the curriculum. Art, music and dance can all be woven into the rich tapestry of the teaching-learning process, a point which will be dealt with in detail elsewhere.

But they have to be backed by much more.

Sport, for instance. In most schools, particularly day schools, sport is viewed as an unwelcome intrusion upon the time available for the 'real thing'. Or at best, the 'sports period' allows the school to use the released classroom for some lesson, which would otherwise be difficult to accommodate.

The truth, however, is that sport, if done seriously can teach life skills that perhaps no classroom can. The skills of teamwork, leadership, losing with grace, winning with humility, playing fair, respect for the opponent—all these and much more that are so badly required in adult life, can be taught by a well-crafted and well-delivered sports programme.

Rajdeep Sardesai, in his book on cricket, *Democracy's XI*[6], quotes Nelson Mandela at the historic 1995 World Cup in South Africa: 'Sport has the power to change the world. It has the power to inspire. It has the power to unite people in a way that little else does. It speaks to youth in a language they understand. Sport can create hope where once there was only despair. It is more powerful than government in breaking down racial barriers.'

Across the world, and surprisingly in our own country, we see that sportspersons are held to a different moral standard altogether. It is acceptable for politicians to be corrupt, for bureaucrats, too, and for business people to be involved in scams, but the moment a sportsperson is found guilty on any count of dishonesty all hell breaks loose. This is why the match-fixing scandal in cricket evoked so much shock and

---

[6]Sardesai, Rajdeep, *Democracy's XI: The Great Indian Cricket Story*, 2017, New Delhi, Juggernaut Books.

dismay. It was just not cricket!

Sport is not only a very powerful weapon to wield in the crusade for honesty of the highest order, but for a variety of critical life skills as well. In order to reap this benefit, however, we must select and train our sports teachers (just as we should do the others), and treat them with respect. As things stand, most schools are quite happy to recruit anyone who remotely fills the bill as a 'sports teacher', and give them a one-point agenda: 'Make sure the school wins all the inter-school tournaments!'

Bereft of any sensitization to issues such as honesty, integrity and fair play, the hapless sports teacher sets out on this mission with a demonic zeal because they know that success will ensure job stability and perhaps more. And the result is what we often see in most inter-school tournaments—fudged birth certificates, complaints, squabbles and, often, violent fights. Sport is usually the loser.

In many schools, it is also the practice to hand over 'discipline' to the sports department. This is because it is believed that the more muscle power used, the better the discipline will be. Teachers who find themselves hopelessly ill-equipped to take on the challenges posed by young adolescents are only too happy to abrogate this responsibility and the results can be, and often are, disastrous. A serious undercurrent of 'dadagiri' (bullying) and gangsterism often pervades the culture of such schools.

The matter is further worsened by the fact that most principals have by and large, no real background in, or appreciation and understanding of, the world of sport. They view it as a necessary evil, or in the best-case scenario, as an instrument to win laurels for, and enhance the market value of, the school.

As a matter of fact, whilst helping some schools recruit for the principal's position, I never fail to be depressed by the number of boring CVs that I come across. Yes, they have all done the statutory Masters of Arts (MA) and Bachelors of Education (BEd). Many even have Doctor of Philosophy degrees or PhDs. They all proudly enumerate the courses and workshops they have attended. But it is very rare to come across anyone who has 'broken away' and done something exciting with his/her life. No risks taken, no charting of unknown paths—and yet these are the people tasked with 'igniting' young minds!

It has been my personal experience, that if a teacher or a Head of school is actively involved in the sports programme, or indeed in any co-curricular activity that the students can have access to, it enables a great deal of bonding with the students. My own mentor, Shomie Das, was passionate about astronomy, and it was not uncommon to see him with a group of students, star-gazing late into the night. If we are not multidimensional ourselves, how can we expect our students to be so?

Being a runner, I trained regularly with the athletes in the school, in addition to competing with them, till such time that a heart condition rendered that impossible. Some of the relationships developed whilst running together have survived to this day.

When the doctors ruled that I could not run, I took to horse riding, as the school that I then headed had a riding programme, which was gasping to be resurrected. The story of that resurrection could probably make a book by itself, but to cut a long story short, starting with three retired broken-down army horses (that had to be put out of their misery), we developed a first-rate professional stable with twenty thoroughbreds, trained for competitive equestrian sport by the students themselves, and backed by a handsome sponsorship that allowed every child in the school to ride, free of cost, if they so desired.

Over 250 students opted for the activity, and it was a matter of time before the school won laurels in the sport not only at the national, but also at the international level. And it was also a matter of time before the students invited their counterparts from the nearby school for the physically challenged so as to instil in them the self-confidence and self-esteem that those children so badly needed. Needless to say, huge lessons were learnt in empathy and caring.

The entire exercise of building the equestrian establishment from scratch and riding and competing together, fostered some unique bonds. I remember one winter we were competing in the national championships at Delhi. The President's Bodyguard had very kindly agreed to host us, and all of us shared tents in that bitter Delhi winter, partook of the food cooked for the troops and, of course, rode together and looked after our horses.

On another occasion, the entire team and its steeds (twelve of them), travelled all the way from Ooty to Shillong. It was an epic rail/truck journey, and the students spent most of their time (including the nights), in the railway wagons, although they had been booked in the air-conditioned carriage. The multiplicity of lessons learnt about caring, sharing, taking responsibility and working together would, I daresay, fill a book. The fact that both my wife, Indrani, and I were with the students on every step of this journey, fostered unbreakable ties and, in turn, helped us to reach out to the larger student community.

And it is not as if only a sport like horse riding can provide such unique opportunities. At another school that I headed, basketball occupied the centre stage of the school's sports programme. It so happened that one year we fought our way into the finals of the most prestigious tournament in the district to find ourselves pitted against our formidable rival school, and a school with an immense reputation.

I had planned to take our whole school (about 600 students) to cheer our team, after carefully sensitizing them about the need for decorum and dignity. The Head of the rival school got wind of our plan and called me to say that he had put a cap of a hundred on the number of students we could bring (the game was being played on their courts), as he feared larger numbers might lead to an ugly confrontation.

All my pleas that I undertook guarantee of the good conduct of my students, fell on deaf ears. Some quick thinking had to be done. As I reflected on my fellow Head's words, I realized that a cap had been put only on the number of students who could attend as spectators. There was no mention of others. I quickly galvanized the entire teaching faculty and the administrative staff, and together we formed a band of nearly three hundred enthusiastic supporters!

The match was played with great enthusiasm, and the cheering was equally, if not more, enthusiastic. We won in the veritable dying seconds of the game—by a single point! I will never forget the sight of the three hundred of us swarming on to the court and lifting our victorious team on to our shoulders. It is difficult to imagine a more 'come together' moment!

Sport, and indeed other outdoor activities like picnics, treks and camps are just one way to bridge the gap between teacher and taught. One of the most wonderful ways by which a community can bond together is by laughing together, and by laughing at our own selves rather than others. Shomie Das (at the Doon School, where he was the Head, and I a teacher) used to encourage the students to imitate him on Teachers' Day. Shomie would sit in the front row when the performance was on, and keel over with laughter at the spoofs the students put up.

Of course, the faculty responded appropriately, which resulted in a great deal of bonhomie on Children's Day—without any offence being caused to either party. I took this practice with me to all the schools that I headed and the results were memorable. I remember being accosted once by the owner of a restaurant on a highway, with the question, 'Aren't you the Head of X school? I recognize you from the video of the Children's Day programme my son brought back from school. We have not stopped laughing over it!'

As a matter of fact, I took this 'culture of laughter' (if one may call it that), a step further and played (and almost invariably successfully) an April Fool's joke on the school each year. The students also got away with some very imaginatively conceived pranks on me, and it was all in good spirit and taste.

Opportunities to 'lighten up' the atmosphere and make school fun exist at all times, and one does not have to wait for Children's Day or April Fool's Day to make it happen. The simple expedient of teachers and students putting up a music show, dance recital, art exhibition or sporting fixtures together, can generate much genuine goodwill and camaraderie.

As can an atmosphere of 'caring' created by a Head, by not making faculty or students wait interminably for an appointment, but by giving them top priority, by reaching out both in times of joy and sorrow. It is also too easy in the 'sellers market' of education, for a Head to cultivate an image of aloofness and behave, particularly with parents and faculty, in a way that suggests that by deigning to meet them, one is doing them a favour. But if the school is to build genuine partnerships, which, in my opinion, is a must for the happy passage of a child through school, then I am afraid that such an attitude will not do. Of course the thin line between a respectful partnership and an unhealthy familiarity must at all times, be maintained. And this is where the Head's social and interpersonal skills will be seriously tested.

All said and done, a school must be a happy place, a place where all stakeholders—parents, students, faculty and support staff—feel supported and welcomed. It does not necessarily take the hosting of mega events with celebrities in attendance to create such a happy atmosphere. Rather, it is the small things that we do, on a day-to-day basis which make all involved feel valued. And a 'happy' school goes a long way towards ensuring that the goals of education are met.

6

Where Are We Heading?

If one were to go by media discussions and reports alone, it would seem that education is one of the most frequently discussed issues on public platforms today—as indeed it should be. The critical question that, however, remains is, how much of this discussion translates into meaningful educational reform?

That reform is a must is undeniable. Today we have the spectre of hundreds of schools springing up all over our cities—international schools, global schools, world schools, English-medium schools, air-conditioned schools, gurukuls, missionary schools, and what-have-you. What is it that they are delivering? Are they really preparing our children to take on the challenges posed by the world that awaits them outside the school walls? And whilst our city schools continue to try and outstrip each other in terms of the luxuries they can provide to their students, what about those in the remote rural areas? They continue to survive with barely a roof over their heads, errant (or worse, drunken) teachers, little or no furniture…

The hard facts stare at us in the face. In an article[7] in

---

[7]Subramanian, T.S.R., 'Not for the Children', *The Indian Express*, 27 June 2017; https://indianexpress.com/article/opinion/columns/not-for-the-children-indian-education-system-4723452/

The Indian Express, T.S.R. Subramanian, former Cabinet Secretary, wrote:

> In December last year the PEW Research Centre in New York, a think-tank focusing on public issues released a research study, with findings of a comparison of schooling in over 90 countries. The study, 'Region and Education Around the World' focuses on 'educational attainment' in the world, and the Indian school educational system is at the bottom of the international league, along with Sub-Saharan Africa... The bad news does not end there. The Annual Status of Education Report conducted by Pratham, an Indian NGO with some credibility, had assessed in 2014 that 75 per cent of all children in class 3, over 50 per cent in class 5 and over 25 per cent in class 8 could not read text books meant for class 2... A recent study in Delhi has come out with the finding that only 54 per cent of the city's children read something—it could be only a sentence. One will have to be extremely obtuse to not realize that the Indian school education system is in terrible shape—even if it is not the worst in the world.

A sad state of affairs indeed!

In a powerfully argued article in *Seminar* magazine (June 2018), Dr Krishna Kumar has sought to give a different perspective to the findings of agencies such as ASER (Annual Status of Education Report) Centre.

According to Dr Kumar, the problem with these findings is that they see the problem of Indian education as a 'crisis of learning'; however, the real problem, argues Dr Kumar, is that it is a 'crisis of teaching'. This understanding enables us to shift our focus to 'unhappy and angry teachers across the country, particularly in North India where the problem is graver'.

There is, to begin with, argues Dr Kumar, a serious paucity of teachers. Around a million teaching posts in our government schools still lie vacant! Schools try and cope with this problem with various 'knee-jerk' solutions, but there can be no getting away from the fact that the impact of this paucity on the learning process is quite devastating.

Moreover, 'applicants for teaching positions have degrees from certified institutions, but a majority of them are academically hollow, and even fraudulent'. Dr Kumar goes on to point out the uncomfortable truth that the quality of knowledge imparted in most of our universities to undergraduates and graduates is so poor, that one shudders to think of what they, in turn, impart to the students entrusted to their care in schools.

Moreover, how many of our teachers are passionate about the subject they teach? For the most part, they themselves had opted for the course at university for reasons far removed from an interest in the subject, and their boredom with, and indifference to, what they teach, comes through very strongly in the classroom. The impact of this on the young mind can be disastrous.

On the other hand, imagine what a fire a teacher like the one enacted by Robin Williams in the movie, *Dead Poets Society*, or, indeed, Sidney Poitier in *To Sir, with Love*, could light in the students' minds?

Add to this, boredom with one's subject and, indeed, career, and the growing belief that training makes no difference—and you have a heady cocktail for disaster.

Dr Kumar goes on to make the powerful argument that there must be a link between the decline of the status of teachers as employees and children's academic performance. Yet we have blissfully ignored the negative impact of decisions taken in several states over the last three decades in matters such as teacher recruitment and their emoluments—policies such as contractual appointments and lowering the status and salary of teachers.

We can formulate, discuss and debate all kinds of educational policies, but unless we look at some of the basic, no progress, I am afraid, is possible on this vital issue.

And at the forefront is the issue of the status of the teaching profession. There can be no denying the fact that for the most part, school teaching is not a first-choice profession. Part of the reason lies in the comparatively lower financial remuneration that this sector receives. And this despite the fact that the average schoolteacher has a punishing work schedule. More often than not, in the case of a female teacher (and they are in majority), she is also a mother and a homemaker, with all the onerous responsibilities that those roles demand, particularly in a country steeped in patriarchy. Add to that the burden of teaching, correcting, setting assignments and tests, filling in reports, commuting to school and back—it really seems a miracle that an individual can roll all this up into a single day! Is it any wonder then that our system lacks creativity? Where is the time and energy to be creative?

Having said that, we still have our fair share of hugely creative and committed teachers, right across the board, down to the municipal schools. Imagine how many more we would have if the ecosystem was supportive?

The bigger problem, of course, is society's attitude to the teaching profession. I remember asking an assembly of parents at a boarding school I was heading, how many of them would like to see their son become a schoolteacher or their daughter marry one? No marks for the correct answer!

On another occasion, I was watching as parents came to pick up their wards for the summer vacation. One father who had come in a particularly impressive car, was taking his leave from his son's housemaster (who was also the maths teacher), when he turned around to the son and counselled: 'You had better study hard in the vacation,' and pointing to the teacher, 'or else you will end up like him!' We just need to take a look around us to see how many children from families that we know, will ever opt for school teaching as a profession. I cannot think of a single school where career counsellors hold out school teaching as a viable career option to the students (they would probably lose their jobs if they did!) Unless societal attitudes change, there is very little hope.

And societal attitudes are quite naturally reflected in management attitudes. Recently, whilst helping out with a private school, I was horrified to see that the bus driver earned more than some of the teachers. When I suggested to the management that they might want to improve their teachers' salaries, their response was that whilst there were a large number of unemployed housewives queuing up to teach, good drivers were difficult to come by!

The problem is further compounded by the fact that we do not look after those who *do* become teachers, either financially or in terms of their training. It is a sad fact that seventy years after Independence, we do not have a single teacher training institute of the stature of say an IIM or an IIT. What we do have is a chain of rather dubious BEd institutes, most of whose credentials are not worth the paper they are written on.

And yet, schoolteachers are supposed to, and do, provide the launch pad for all professions! What an incredible responsibility!

The sad fact is that teachers are supposed to learn 'on the job' and generations of children have to suffer the 'learning pangs'! I wonder if the army would dispatch a recruit to the front and ask him to learn on the job? Learning on the job also means that one's learning process is totally in the hands of the management of the school. One has to be exceptionally lucky in this country to find a far-sighted management that will recognize this need and respond.

Even a well-meaning and progressive management these days finds the waters muddied by the constant threat of governmental interference. Gurcharan Das, in a brilliant article[8] in the TOI, has made an incisive analysis of this current predicament education finds itself in. The Right to Education (RTE) Act insists that private schools maintain parity with government schools in the matter of teacher salaries. The same law insists that 25 per cent of the students in the school must come from poor families. Though in theory, the government is supposed to pay the fees of all poor students, the fact is that rarely happens. What this means is that the full-fee paying

---

[8] Das, Gurcharan, 'Why governments shouldn't mess with private school fees', *The Times of India*, 6 August 2017; https://blogs.timesofindia.indiatimes.com/men-and-ideas/why-governments-shouldnt-mess-with-private-school-fees/

students (the 75 per cent) have to cover the cost of both the enhanced teacher salaries and the fee deficit of the 25 per cent.

Where does the hapless management find the money? They have to perforce raise the fees. This brings in its wake a furious backlash from the parents. Protests erupt. The management has to dramatically prune other costs, and the axe falls on critical areas such as teacher training, infrastructure, student safety. As Gurcharan Das points out, those managements not willing to compromise on these essentials simply close down, and yet another potentially good school bites the dust.

The answer to this problem, Das goes on to argue, lies in the model provided by the Self-financed Independent Schools Act, 2017, of Andhra Pradesh, which encourages private schools to open, gives them freedom of admission and fees and removes corruption from the board of affiliation (this, to my mind, is easier said than done, and is probably where the entire exercise can either succeed or fail).

Das goes on to add the rider that schools, once given this freedom must exercise it responsibly by providing in a completely transparent manner, on the school's website, all details such as fees, staff qualifications, details of infrastructure strengths and weaknesses—everything that a parent needs to know before selecting a school. With competition, Das argues, fee control becomes unnecessary.

There is solid merit in this argument. I am no economist, but judging by the way, say the technology market has responded to competition, I daresay we may see a replication of what is happening there—a plethora of choices, and at an affordable cost.

To cut back, however, to the problem of the paucity

of teachers. Since the pool of teachers is a small one, is it surprising that the pool of potential heads of schools is even smaller? And to make matters worse, there are no training programmes for Heads either. Heads are, for the most part, 'teachers on promotion', who are left to fend for themselves. This is a subject to be dealt with on its own elsewhere.

If the education system is to become truly a world-class one, it has to become an 'aspirational' one—one that young people would see as being a genuinely worthwhile goal. Perhaps one of the steps that could be taken would be to create a pan-India merit-based service for teachers along the lines of the civil services (minus its faults, of course). As in Finland, one must prove oneself worthy of being a teacher, rather than walk off the street into the job, as is the case in India today. Of course schools today do conduct interviews for teachers. But how much of a choice do they really have?

A well-trained, well-paid and respected force of teachers would also be imbued with a sense of professional pride—something that the profession lacks badly. How many of our teachers read—anything, leave alone matters related to their profession? How many of our teachers are genuinely proud of their profession and, more importantly, reflect that pride in the daily execution of their duties? And yet they are entrusted with the task of inspiring young minds to learn!

As Dr Krishna Kumar has pointed out, the bedrock on which the entire education system rests is the teacher. And there is a multiplicity of issues involved here. Merely setting up a chain of BEd institutes will not do. Society (and this includes civil society and government) will have to look at the profession through a totally different set of lenses. This, in turn, will involve revisiting recruitment, emoluments, training and imparting a hugely better quality of higher education. In short, a veritable revolution.

I will not forget what I said to a promoter who had recruited me to set up a new school outside Dehradun. He was waxing eloquent about the technology his proposed school would boast of—Internet (VoIP) phones, toilets with sensors, classrooms with the latest gizmos and even a helipad!

My answer to him was very simple, 'Give me half a dozen teachers excited about learning and who love to work with young minds, a tree to provide shelter and a black board, and I will give you a world-class school.' Perhaps I was stretching a point, but then so was he! Needless to say, we soon parted company.

The other vital component of the system is, of course, the curriculum. Where do we stand on this crucial issue? I am no great expert on curriculum, but it seems to me that the entire conceptual framework of our curriculum, be it the national or state boards, is based on erroneous assumptions.

'Education', by its very definition, is meant to open up the mind. All our curricula are designed just to do the opposite. At a very early stage, right from Class IX onwards, we start boxing in young minds into watertight compartments of 'science', 'commerce' and, at the bottom of the caste system, the 'humanities'. Whereas education should be all about letting the mind wander, explore, see and marvel at the connections between different phenomena, what we do is to imprison the mind and bombard it with often irrelevant information that goes under the disguise of 'syllabus'. Take away the textbook and the average teacher will be left rudderless.

This kind of sequestered thinking stems from the belief

that almost from Class IX onwards, a child should make up their mind about a choice of career. And what is the career that tops the aspiration list? Engineering, of course, followed closely by Information Technology (IT), medicine and business management. The fact that we live in such a fast-changing world, where almost anything you do, if you do it well, can become a career, is lost upon our planners. After all, whoever thought, not so long ago, that river-rafting and wildlife photography could be serious options? And equally importantly, who can say ten years down the line, what new possibilities will exist?

Author and education specialist, Sir Ken Robinson, in one of his famous Ted Talks ('Do schools kill creativity?'), points out that the child who is enrolling in school today is most likely to retire sixty-five years from now. At the rate the world is changing, we do not even know what the world will be like in terms of careers five years down the line, leave alone sixty-five years along the road! So how can the conventional educational system, with its emphasis on reproducing content taught in the classroom, prepare the children for this uncertain and challenging future?

What the system *should* do is to foster creativity and the questioning mind that is inherent in the child, so that s/he is well-equipped to adapt to rapidly changing circumstances. What we are doing today is, however, just the opposite—we stifle creativity and discourage the questioning mind. And if this is a criticism of what is happening in the West, one shudders to think what Sir Robinson would think of what is happening in India!

Art, music and dance, for instance, which could be used as

powerful pedagogical instruments, are relegated to the position of 'second-class' citizens in the school's scheme of things. And the responsibility for teaching these disciplines is handed over to 'part-time' teachers who are usually squeezed in during the after-class hours, and find even that little time taken away if the school has other priorities on the day. The fact is, however, that in the hands of an imaginative teacher these can become the fulcrum of the teaching-learning process.

A middle school history teacher I know, whilst teaching her young pupils about the Stone Age, roped in the art department of the school to create artefacts resembling those of the period she was teaching. She then requisitioned the assistance of some of the older students to dig a pit where these artefacts could be buried. The middle schoolers were then informed that an archaeological site had been located on the campus and that they were to excavate at that site.

The local archaeological department was asked to instruct the budding archaeologists on the techniques of safe excavation. Some of the pupils were assigned the task of being journalists who would cover the event. What resulted that day was a veritable 'jamboree' of learning, where a huge amount of fun was had, and many skills were learnt. No great financial outlay was required. It was just a bit of imagination, common sense and team work.

And yet we continue to plod on with rote learning. What we fail to realize is that rote learning, which seems to be the norm in most schools, deadens the mind to the extent that in adult life, a mind desensitized by rote, unquestioningly accepts much of what is hurled at it, including very often messages of hate, prejudice and violence. This is certainly not the basis for a successful and genuine democracy.

And, of course, this obsession with the so-called prestigious professional courses provides the lifeblood of the 'tuition centres', which are perhaps the most pernicious aspect of this entire scenario. Like leeches, they suck the life out of childhood. Much like conveyor belts, they churn out minds equipped solely with the ability to tackle entrance examinations. The power of these sweat shops is so great that often teachers do not deliberately teach in the classroom, but refer their students to their centres for the 'real thing'! There are also schools, which, in their quest for top results, skip the Class XI syllabus and finish the Class XII portion a year earlier. Quite akin to fattening an animal for slaughter by force—feeding it with steroids!

The TOI (18 October 2017) reported the alarming findings of the Assocham Survey (2013), the highlights of which were:

1) Close to 87% of primary and 95% of higher secondary students attend private coaching classes.
2) Over 85% of parents think that they are ill-equipped or lack time to teach children on their own.
3) Statistics reveal that middle-class parents have been spending one-third of their monthly income on their children's private tuition.
4) Private tutors charge anything between ₹1,000/ to ₹4,000/ per hour per student on a one-to-one basis.
5) Group tuition costs ₹1,000/ to ₹6,000/ a month.
6) 78% of parents spend ₹1,000/ to ₹3,000/ a month on tuitions for a primary school ward.
7) Parents spend above ₹5,000/ a month for the tuitions of a secondary level child.

We have, knowingly, committed our children to a vicious cycle of school-tuition-examination that completely stifles creativity, kills their imagination, destroys their childhood and, very often, makes them incapable of contributing to a genuinely democratic system.

'Education', in the Indian scenario has, sadly, been reduced to the proverbial 'tamasha' or spectacle. The announcement of board examination results is greeted each year by billboards, advertisements and TV shows loudly hailing the 'toppers'. Marks are distributed like sweets at a wedding. One of the saddest fallouts of this jamboree is that we are not teaching our children to accept, respect and learn from failure. Woe betide the child who, for whatever reason—be it a learning disability, lack of opportunity or poor health—cannot make it to the 90 per cent bracket, leave alone fail.

In the hullabaloo of celebrating the success stories, these unfortunate souls must want the earth to open up and swallow them. And the sad truth is that many of them *do*—by committing suicide! The fact that all of them are gifted in some area which conventional examinations can never reveal, is of no consequence. They will remain children of a lesser god, unless some rare stroke of luck comes their way. Not even the disturbing number of suicides at the Mecca of tuitions—Kota (in Rajasthan)—can force us to reflect on the absurdity and cruelty of our system.

The group that suffers the most in this mad race for marks is children with learning disabilities. And there are, indeed, a disturbing number of them out there. The tragedy is that most schools do not even have the wherewithal to spot them, leave alone help. Moreover, teachers are so busy churning out 90-percenters (because their increments and, often, jobs depend on the success stories) that these children fall through the cracks and are more often than not branded as 'plain stupid'. When I started an Assisted Learning Centre for children with disabilities in one of the public schools I headed, one of my Board members gravely warned me of the dangers of taking on 'mentally retarded' children!

With our obsession with training our young from such an early age to be 'professionals', how successful have we been in even achieving this goal?

A recent report[9] in the *Hindustan Times* says that, 'Indian millennials are not equipped with the skills they need to be successful in the careers of tomorrow, according to a survey conducted by HBR Ascend, an online learning companion for millennials.' The report goes on to say, 'The survey highlights the lack of four skills in millennials today that are critical in dealing with the vulnerabilities of the workplace—emotional intelligence, stress management, persuasion and analytical thinking.' Perhaps, if we had focused on imparting a genuine education, instead of obsessing with 'professional' courses, we could have avoided this pitfall.

Author and education specialist, Tony Wagner, in his path-breaking work, *The Global Achievement Gap*,[10] discusses in detail the seven essential skills required for success in today's world. These are, in Wagner's opinion: critical thinking

---

[9]'Indian millennials lack critical skills: HBR Ascend survey', *Hindustan Times*, 18 July 2017.
[10]Wagner, Tony, *The Global Achievement Gap: Why Even Our Best Schools Don't Teach the New Survival Skills Our Children Need—And What We Can Do About It*, 2008, New York, Basic Books.

and problem-solving; collaboration across networks and leading by influence; agility and adaptability; initiative and entrepreneurialism; effective oral and written communication skills; accessing and analysing information; curiosity and imagination. In the Indian context, I would like to add an eighth—empathy and tolerance. How these skills are to be delivered would be a subject for a book entirely devoted to pedagogy.

Closely related to this obsession with seeing school education primarily as a gateway to professional courses, has been the steady denigration of the humanities. It is a standard practice in most schools to offer the sciences to those who are seen as high achievers, commerce to the average ones and the humanities to those who are perceived as not good enough for the first two.

Teachers openly stigmatize those who are either offered, or even opt for the humanities. Some schools do not even bother with the option of the humanities! What is totally overlooked is that a student, despite a high percentage achieved in Class X, may not have an inclination, or indeed aptitude, for the sciences, whereas a student with a comparatively low grade may have an inborn scientific bent of mind.

In any case, the Class X examination is a bit of a farce, and besides the fact that it bears no relationship to what is taught in Classes XI and XII, is a poor indicator of a student's aptitude or abilities, and more of a test of rote-learning skills.

The bigger point is that no one seems to realize one fundamental truth: no matter what career one decides to pursue—be it engineering, medicine, software technology, or what have you—one needs to have a world view, an understanding of peoples, of value systems, of how societies evolve and what makes them tick. And, most importantly, we must endow our children with the gift of imagination. This is perhaps what the late President A.P.J. Abdul Kalam had in mind when he spoke of 'igniting the mind'.

This is the classical humanist spirit that drove the Renaissance, and that is why the West has not abandoned the humanities in the way we have done. Oxford and Cambridge, of course, stand out as beacons in this respect, and the PPE (Politics, Philosophy, Economics) undergraduate programmes continue to attract the finest minds. American universities, too, insist on students doing 'technical courses' also coupling them with a liberal arts programme. All good school boards, whether it is the International Baccalaureate, the IGCSE or the A levels, give pride of place to the humanities.

It cannot be debated that an education that fails to sensitize young minds to art, poetry, literature, people and society, can at best produce technicians and workers—not leaders. For leaders must be imbued with a vision. And a vision is possible only if one's learning combines the understanding of the nitty-gritty with a larger understanding and appreciation of the nuances of the world we live in.

Of late, there has been a great deal of discussion in the media about the 'shrinking space' for debate and dissent. What is shrinking is not only the space but also our hearts and minds.

The CBSE has taken a bold step in revitalizing the social studies curriculum. But apart from the fact that very often, successive governments see the social sciences as an ideological weapon, the delivery of the humanities remains in the hands of boring, cynical teachers. After all, there is not much of a tuition market for these subjects!

What is urgently required is a thorough relook at the way in which we view school education. First and foremost, we must stop viewing it as a means to an entry into any particular career. What it must do, is to equip our young with the skills of literacy and, of course, a sound understanding of the basics of all subjects—be it maths, science, geography, history or literature.

But more importantly, it must equip the young mind with the wherewithal to see the interconnectedness of all knowledge, ask questions, think critically, be a self-learner and problem-solver, enjoy and appreciate the beauty of nature and marvel at the organic relationship between all living beings.

There is this interesting and rather revealing story about the world-famous mathematician Ken Ono and his mentor, Basil Gordon, narrated by Amruta Lakhe in *The Indian Express*.[11]

Ono once wrote, 'I could not wait to start working on theorems but he (Gordon), did not let me anywhere near a math formula for months. We went biking, played the piano, and opened our minds to classical music.' Then on one of their expeditions, Ono was struck by the beauty of the sunset and mentioned it to Gordon. Gordon replied that Ono 'was now ready to do math!'

Krishna Kumar, one of the most eminent educationists in the country, perhaps sums it all up best when he says, 'Our system hates eccentricity, ignores pre-disposition, and punishes single-minded devotion to a particular subject. Education and

---

[11]Lakhe, Amruta, 'Prime Obsession', *The Indian Express*, 8 May 2016; https://indianexpress.com/article/lifestyle/life-style/prime-obsession/

exams seem a burden to so many precisely because everyone is assumed to be alike. The fact that many of our children excel despite the rigidity of our system encourages the popular argument that our system has rigour.'

In order for school education to be viewed as a valuable end in itself, and not as a means to an end, we will have to de-link the process from college admission, as indeed is done in many parts of the world, whereby colleges have independent admission procedures and are linked to school results only in a very basic form. The ridiculous business of unrealistic 'cut-offs' must be terminated. For this to happen, serious reform of higher education, too, is needed, with many more good universities being made available and offering a vast variety of courses.

It also appears to me that precious little is being done in this country to foster genuine research in school education. The odd researcher here and there publishes the odd PhD that is soon buried amongst millions of such tomes. The bulk of the research work is left to a government-controlled body called the National Council of Educational Research and Training (NCERT), which must necessarily toe the current dispensation's line. Unfortunately, teachers who must be in the forefront of research have neither the time and ability nor, indeed, inclination to add to the burden they already carry. This state of affairs does not portend well for the future or, indeed, the present.

There also seems to be a belief amongst many of our school promoters that the more 'high-tech' a school, the more of an 'international' image it will carry. There can be no doubt that technology is a great enabler when it comes to education.

Some have even gone so far to suggest an ethnography app that lets children record their stimuli, perhaps incorporating audio recording or video/photo capture and field notes, and a cloud-based repository that can be retrieved by a hashtag.

There are, however, serious dangers that lurk with an undue emphasis on technology. First of all, in a country like India where a huge number of schools are struggling to just acquire a blackboard, it can exacerbate the already yawning gap between the haves and the have-nots. The injudicious use of technology can also make children more inward-looking and, perhaps, selfish. I saw this in the US where students who were sitting across each other at the dining table, would communicate with each other by texting rather than speaking! Is the 'selfie' generation that we are producing going to turn into a 'selfish' generation? And of course, technology when taken to an extreme, can 'dehumanize' the education process. After all there is no substitute for the teacher who can put her or his arm around a student's shoulders and say, for instance, 'Hey, it is okay to fail' or indeed discuss the difference between right and wrong.

The debate about the direction in which our system is going, or indeed where it should go is a never-ending one, as indeed it should be. The human mind is extremely dynamic, and understanding how it learns is a very complex and ongoing process. Having said that, it is about time that school education was put on the front burner. Every politician and, indeed, dignitary invited to a school function, will at some point in the speech remind children that the future of this great country lies in their hands. If that is true, we had better start putting our money where our mouths are.

7

From Cocoon to Butterfly

When the ten plus two system was introduced in our country, it was the fond hope of the planners that this move would ease the pressure on the higher education system. The thought was that only those students genuinely interested in pursuing higher education would opt for the 'academic' courses on offer in Classes XI and XII. The rest would opt for the plethora of 'vocational' courses made available, and avoid crowding the universities, taking up these alternative courses instead.

Unfortunately, the hopes of our planners were belied. In a country obsessed with degrees, this was hardly likely to happen. Parents, students and, indeed, employers could not envisage a future for anyone not in possession of a degree. Everyone thus continued to see school education as a 'certification process', for entrance to university, the university as an essential step to a degree, and a degree as a passport to a job.

It is not uncommon for parents to ask, 'Should I put my child into a CBSE or an ISC school? I have been told that the CBSE prepares students better for entrance to the IITs.' In other words, parents often decide to put their child into a school for one reason only: to crack the IIT system, and the boards seem happy to oblige.

Whilst, to my mind, there is a fundamental flaw in treating school education as a mere certification process (a point on which I have dwelt in detail in an earlier chapter), the fact is that this system is unlikely to change in the foreseeable future. Which then brings us to another big problem. How prepared are our children for the world of university, and equally importantly, how prepared are the universities for the school-leaver?

P. Chidambaram, in an article[12] in *The Indian Express*, has opined, 'A university is not a mere collection of buildings. It is also not a collection of colleges or centres of research. It is not constituted solely for the purpose of conferring degrees upon young men and women who enter its portals, study subjects and pass examinations. It is a space designed to nurture knowledge and freedom, and beckon the children of the world to take from, and give unto the reservoir of knowledge and freedom.'

If this is indeed true, how prepared are our school-leavers to take on this new ecosystem? A good university would ideally look for good 'self-learners', critical thinkers, students who can think laterally, and ask questions. But what we have done in our schools is, ironically, just the opposite. We compartmentalize children in 'knowledge boxes' from a very early stage, and discourage a spirit of inquiry as it interferes with success in examinations. How often have I heard the lament, 'X is a hugely disruptive element in my class. He is forever asking questions!'

---

[12]Chidambaram, P., 'Across the aisle: From university to mediocrity', *The Indian Express*, 27 February 2017; https://indianexpress.com/article/opinion/columns/across-the-aisle-from-university-to-mediocrity-jnu-harvard-ramjas-colllege-iisc-iit-ugc-4543800/

We have bombarded young minds with tuitions and training for cracking the various entrance examinations, and deadened all their creativity and critical thinking abilities. As a matter of fact, it is perfectly possible for a student these days to register as a 'ghost candidate' in a school in order to secure the attendance required to sit the board examination, and carry on merrily at a tuition centre miles away from that school!

From this highly structured world of 'spoon-feeding', the unsuspecting young soul is catapulted into the world of university, so eloquently described by P. Chidambaram, where there are minimal structures and a bewildering array of choices.

The problem is far greater for those attending foreign universities. We get to know of, and celebrate, only the success stories amongst Indian students in foreign universities, many of whom have been to school in those countries anyway. We very rarely, if ever, hear of the sad stories of those who fail to make the cut on account of a total lack of preparedness.

From a scenario where there is daily attendance in school, and an accompanying furore if one even misses a single class, the adolescent is, almost overnight, sent into a situation where no one gives two hoots if you attend class or not—until the time of examinations, when a shortage of attendance can prove to be disastrous.

The expectations and delivery mechanisms in the classroom, too, are very different. Whereas the schoolteacher would probably spend some time and effort to explain a difficult concept (if only to ensure that his class results do not dip), or perhaps refer the troubled student to his tuition centre after school hours, the college lecturer is bound by no such obligation.

The average college lecturer (in a reasonably good college that is), would probably breeze into the classroom, deliver a lecture (or more fashionably a 'presentation') and then breeze out, leaving behind a long reading list. For our spoon-fed school-leaver, this can be a hugely disorienting experience.

The confusion, and often a sense of alienation, is not limited to the classroom. It permeates all aspects of university life. Many schools are single-sex—most universities are not. This has its own challenges for the young mind. Even those who come from mixed schools (where very strict rules regarding gender mixing exist) have problems dealing with the freedom of gender interaction that most universities allow, because universities work on the assumption that they are dealing with 'adults', whereas our school-leaver is actually far from being one.

Quite recently, I witnessed first-hand in a 'global university' that I worked in as Director, Student Welfare, the conflict generated by the clash of 'global' values in the matter of attire and interaction between the sexes and the 'traditional' values in the case of those who hailed from more conservative backgrounds. In my capacity as the chairperson of the Disciplinary Committee at the university, I had to once deal with a situation where a young man had tried to smuggle a young lady into the men's hostel in a suitcase! The situation appeared to be quite amusing until one reflected on the possible consequences of this Galahad's actions in a deeply patriarchal society; consequences of the kind, which, indeed, the very same university had experienced earlier. And, believe me, that had been no laughing matter.

Schools are, by and large, rather homogenous in terms of their student population—universities are not. A university is a huge 'melting pot', with students from almost all states and backgrounds finding representation there. This is indeed a great strength of the university. But for our already overawed, confused school-leaver, this heterogeneity presents its own challenges, and coping can be quite painful.

Also, making the right choice of group to 'hang out' with is not easy, and hitherto 'forbidden fruit' is all too tempting for the impressionable mind. It was saddening to see how many first-year students found themselves being hauled up in front of the Disciplinary Committee for various forms of transgressions, ranging from poor attendance, to smuggling in cigarettes and alcohol, to sexual harassment, serious substance abuse and, indeed, gang warfare!

The truth is that the move from the protected environs of the school where almost every decision is taken for you (life is run by the school bell, as some put it), to this seemingly 'free-for-all' environment, with apparently unlimited choices, is a hugely difficult one. It can also lead to serious problems of loneliness and depression.

And how equipped are our universities to guide the young school-leaver through this veritable minefield? Having decided that they are dealing with 'adults', most universities could not care less. And it suits their revenue model as well, not to have to invest in what they consider a 'non-main line' activity. The focus is on getting in the numbers—not on looking after them.

To begin with, most residential universities commit their wards to the care of 'wardens'. By definition, wardens belong to jails or, at best, wildlife reserves! They can certainly not be expected to guide the new entrants through what is probably the most challenging phase of their lives. First of all, they rarely possess the educational qualifications required for such a sensitive appointment. For the most part they are retired service personnel, or ex-security personnel, no doubt equipped with a host of skills, but not always the ones appropriate to the task in hand. Asking them to handhold the young 'freshers' is akin to asking a tonga horse to compete in the Kentucky Derby! To allocate resources for recruiting and training personnel who would enjoy the near status of teaching faculty, is something most universities would not even dream of.

My recent experience of two kinds of 'higher educational' set-ups will perhaps demonstrate the point I am trying to make. The first relates to the proliferation of 'private' institutes that flourish in the Doon valley where I live, and is no doubt replicated over most of the country.

All these institutes claim to be 'recognized' by some organization or the other. Their billboards, advertising their wares, which include dozens of courses ranging from aviation engineering to plant biology to oceanography, and their claims to 'five-star' infrastructure, dot the entire landscape. The cost of each course is also clearly spelt out, and placed as they are amongst the billboards of the local eateries, one can be forgiven for confusing one with the other!

I had the dubious distinction of being invited to 'advise' one such institution (and perhaps the biggest of the lot with a student enrolment of over 10,000, spread over three campuses). What I saw and experienced left me quite unnerved.

The students were recruited by touts strategically placed in different and far-flung parts of the country, with an extremely attractive package of allurements. Most of the recruits were from not-so-privileged families, and I came across several cases where the parents had actually sold off their lands to make the dream possible for their child.

And 'dreamers' they certainly were, with the young men determined to be professional IT experts or whatever, and the young girls entertaining visions of becoming air-hostesses or even Bollywood stars. The 'lucky' ones secure admission to the hostels whereas the rest have to fend for themselves in PG accommodation of varying degrees of dubiousness, that have sprouted all over these areas. Fresh from the hinterland, these youngsters have to cope not only with the demands of a strange educational system, but also the shock of an urban culture. Little wonder then that many fall by the wayside.

And what exactly is on offer to them? The quality of hostel life varies from institution to institution. The quality of the rooms available tends to be far from reasonable, as the promoters are acutely aware of the need to cut costs. At the institute that I was asked to advise, the food was cooked in the most unhygienic conditions imaginable. The cooks themselves lived in hovels and used the open fields nearby as a toilet! There was no medical help available other than the statutory first-aid box, and I shuddered to think of the predicament of a student who might fall ill in the middle of the night, as the institute was a fair bit away from the city.

For those living either as paying guests or in rented accommodations, the situation is not much better. Projected into a completely alien world, far removed from the rural hinterland where they come from, bereft of any kind of supervision and often hard up for money, it is all too easy for these young folk to fall right into any one of the numerous pits that surround them.

As for academic concerns… The biggest conundrum to my mind was where the institute secured their faculty from, considering the incredible number of courses on offer, and the fact that the average salary of a lecturer varied from ₹15,000 to ₹17,000 and they had to clock in at 9 a.m. and clock out at 5 p.m.!

One incident gave me some insight into what was, perhaps, happening on a larger scale. One summer day, I was preparing to return home (advise rendered), when I was asked to offer a ride to a young lady (also a lecturer from a similar institution nearby), who had just finished her duties as an 'external examiner' in physics at this particular institute.

On the way back, it being a blistering hot day, the conversation turned to the weather. The radio had just announced the temperatures, and as a conversational gambit, I asked the lady to clear my confusion regarding conversion of centigrade to Fahrenheit. She stuttered in embarrassment, and then confessed, 'I am sorry, I have no idea!'

Cut to the most expensive, state-of-the-art, global private university which would put even some of the finest five-star hotels to shame. Here our concern is with what the jargon terms 'Millennials'—to my mind, for the most part, a group of highly entitled rich young men and women from privileged backgrounds, anxious to cash in on what they perceive as a booming economy, shimmy up the corporate ladder as quickly as they can and live the lifestyles of the 'rich and famous'.

Unfortunately, they too, like their counterparts in the smaller towns described earlier, lack one very essential element for healthy growth. And it is not food that is the missing component. It is a guiding hand. Left to the trusteeship of wardens described earlier, these young souls flounder just as much as their small-town counterparts, with one difference. Whereas their counterparts, say in the Doon valley, suffer from a lack of money and good faculty, the latter suffer from a surfeit of both. The elite private universities have spared no effort to garner the services of top-class faculty from all over the world. That is not the problem—the problem is not in the classroom, it is outside it. Left to their own devices, these impressionable young minds fall prey to a host of pitfalls described earlier.

A common thread that runs through both kinds of institutions, and further aggravates the problem, is the genuine lack of good counsellors in the country. As pointed out earlier, we have steadily denigrated the study of the humanities in our schools. One of the many casualties in this process has been the subject of psychology. It is not taught in most schools, and where it is indeed taught, it is done very badly as there are virtually no psychology teachers available, and schools are forced to resort to the expedient of deputing a teacher with reasonable English-speaking skills to teach the subject.

Moreover, there are not many universities that offer this subject as well—at least as a well-structured, well-delivered programme. When we put all this together, are we surprised that there is a glaring paucity of counsellors (good ones, that is), in the entire country? Universities, too, feel the pinch and, as a result, the already alienated, depressed adolescent, has no one to turn to. I spent most of my time as Director, Student Welfare, just listening to young people unburden themselves.

And the pressures on them are enormous. The pressure to succeed, peer pressure, the pressure of social media—the list is endless. I call them the 'pressure cooker generation'!

Let us also look at the bigger picture. If we indeed agree with P. Chidambaram when he opines about the larger purpose of a university: 'It is a space designed to nurture knowledge and freedom, and beckon the children of the world to take from, and give unto the reservoir of knowledge and freedom,' are we achieving this purpose in either of the two types of institutions that we have examined so far?

In the first case, the students' sole purpose is survival, and not anything lofty. In the second case, one would expect the millennial, who is well-fed, watered and looked after (once they have settled into college life after surviving the teething pangs), to look at larger issues affecting the lives of one's fellow countrymen perhaps? The only 'student movement' I saw in the university I worked at was a rather militant one, aimed at securing faster Internet speed and better central AC facilities! And thereby hangs a tale!

The greater irony is that the universities where these larger issues are indeed a concern of the students and being debated, run the risk today of being seen as 'anti-national', and threatened with battle tanks to evoke patriotism. Education has 'failed', so bring on the tanks!

Until such time that both schools and universities seriously address this issue of guiding the young school-leaver through at least the initial phase of their university career and teach them to not only cope with the demands of an entirely new stage in their lives, but also figure out what it is that they should take out of a system of higher education, our children, and indeed our country, will continue to suffer. We will continue to flounder along, with no real leadership; because, no leadership of any substance can emerge from this system. If it indeed does, it will be despite the system and not because of it.

It is perhaps worth thinking about scrapping the current Class X board examination (it is not taken very seriously anyway) and having the final school-leaving examination in Class XI. Class XII could then be treated as a 'college preparatory year'. The curriculum for this programme could be drawn up in consultation with the universities and, amongst other things, it could hone the skills of the students for self-study, critical thinking, problem-solving and other essential skills required not only for success at university, but in life as well.

There is even the possibility of introducing the school-leaver-to-be to the world of work through well-planned internship programmes. And, of course, for those still obsessed with IITs and the like, more time could be released for serious preparation, instead of falling between the two proverbial stools as they are wont to do at the moment.

Universities, on their parts, would have to elevate pastoral care to nearly the same level as their academic programmes and be prepared to invest in appropriate personnel. This kind of synergy would go a long way towards ensuring a happy, well-balanced and meaningful university life, which in turn might help create a happy, well-balanced and aware citizenry, perhaps even guided by selfless, statesmanlike leaders.

8

The Problem of Principals

It never ceases to amaze me as to how many queries I receive asking me to recommend a Head for a school and it never ceases to amaze me either, when I am left scratching my head for an answer.

This problem has two dimensions. The first and most obvious one (and one which we shall try and address in some detail) is the crying shortage of prospective Heads for schools. But not to be ignored is the fact that even when appropriate candidates are around, one is hesitant to recommend them. This is because most 'promoters', whilst loudly declaring that they are looking for someone whom they wish to grant total autonomy to, are, in fact, looking for just the opposite—they want someone who will quietly 'push the files' and do the management's (very often, family) bidding.

To return to the paucity of principal material in the country. Is it that there is a genuine shortage of appropriate personnel to fill in these posts? Or, is it that the existing personnel are just not good enough? The answer, I suspect, is a bit of both.

As discussed in an earlier chapter, the profession of school teaching, for a host of reasons, does not seem to attract many. The catchment area for likely principals is, therefore, very tiny, even to begin with. Apart from a whole host of reasons, there is also a historical background to this situation.

Right from the days of Nehruvian socialism, school teaching was never thought of as a genuine 'profession'. One taught because it was a 'calling' and did not (or should not) bother too much about earthly matters like wages and remuneration. It was easier to worship the guru, rather than pay him. The emphasis, in the flush of Independence, was to churn out doctors and engineers, who, it was hoped, would rapidly make India catch up with the West, particularly the Soviet Union.

The nation then went into the MBA mode, and before long, the Information Technology revolution took over. School teaching was, therefore, never even deemed a distant prospect. Some from wealthy families went into public school teaching, not because they needed the money, but because these schools offered them a certain lifestyle, whereby they could pursue their hobbies and have no professional pressure to deal with. After all, their students got jobs with their contacts on the golf course and through the 'old boy' tie. The Indian job market was vastly different in those days of innocence. As we know, all that has changed—and how!

Whilst the shortage of teachers for these historical (amongst other) reasons still persists, the story of the metros today is slightly different. Here, there is a huge pool of well-educated talent, particularly amongst housewives seeking a second income. Teaching fits in well into their lifestyles. They are normally out of their homes and back along with their children. The income is very useful, though not critical, and the job keeps them fruitfully occupied and professionally fulfilled.

There is, however, one caveat to this situation. Most of the better educated and well-heeled ladies normally, and for obvious reasons, gravitate to the upper-end schools, whilst the less better off (and perhaps not as highly educated and 'sophisticated') end up in schools where the working conditions and salaries are pitiable. This is, of course, no reflection of their talent, ability or commitment. Of course, not included within the scope of the term 'teaching profession' are the hordes of tutorial academies and 'tuition givers' in all the cities.

Which brings us to a related problem. There is a staggering male–female imbalance in the profession. A leading school recently advertised for teachers. Of the 5,000 applications they received, only twenty or so were from men! Most schools all over the country face a similar situation. Schools that are looking for a male principal because of their own peculiar necessities are, therefore, confronted with a huge predicament. Where have all the good men gone?

Before we actually try and find the root causes for the paucity of Heads, it would be interesting to examine the nature of the role a Head is expected to play. I have already dwelt on the challenging nature of the job in an earlier chapter. What is it that a Head should have, to deal with these challenges?

Gone are the days of Tom Brown's schooldays when it was enough for a Head to be merely a good teacher or, at best, a stern disciplinarian. The increasing complexity of educational administration on account of the huge pressures and demands that the sector faces, means that today's Heads have an extremely demanding job cut out for them—if they desire to be 'leaders' and not just managers doing the management's bidding, that is.

Heads must be in firm control of the strategic direction and development of the school, understand and appreciate the nuances of the teaching-learning process, lead and manage staff effectively, deploy staff and resources, have excellent PR skills and, above all, be accountable. These are only the broad areas that engage their attention. If these are to be broken down into their respective components, the job card of the Head is truly formidable.

In order to be truly effective in the performance of these duties, a good Head must possess a vast range of attributes. And most of these have to be acquired the hard way—ideally through a combination of systematic training and experience (the first of which is unfortunately missing in this country). They must be foremost good teachers. There is no substitute for leadership by reputation and example.

A good Head is necessarily a good leader. That in itself implies the possession of a multiplicity of skills—team building and confidence building being critical. This is something that has been dealt with in detail in an earlier chapter. A Head must realize that for the most part 'readymade' teachers are not available. What is most often available are untrained or badly trained individuals, who are sometimes completely demotivated by their lack of success in other walks of life. It is the Head's job to bring out the best from this resource—to enthuse, inspire and mould this crude clay into a fine sculpture.

Being child-centred is a vital quality for Headship. Heads must constantly search their souls for an answer to the question, 'Do I really enjoy being with young people? Am I passionate about touching their lives?' If the answer is 'no', then one is better off in some other profession. Any Head who cannot empathize with a child's needs, aims, aspirations, joys and sorrows, cannot successfully perform that role.

It is imperative for a Head to be a good communicator. Poor communication ability does not inspire confidence amongst faculty, parents or students. A Head must also have good public relation (PR) skills and be sensitive to the needs and feelings of not only the school community, but also the larger community in which the school is placed.

Unfortunately, because in our country most Heads enjoy the comfort of an unrealistic supply-demand situation in terms of student enrolment (there is invariably a 'waiting list' in most schools), it is all too easy to descend into arrogant and condescending behaviour. And a good Head must always guard against this danger, as such behaviour invariably has deleterious consequences all around.

It goes without saying that a Head must be able to take quick, but well-thought-out decisions, sometimes unpalatable to many. A sharp eye for administration, keeping constant vigil on the overall running of the school and its finances, judicious use of administrative resources—all these go into the 'job card'. And, finally, a good Head must realize that for a school to be truly effective, all its constituencies must have a strong and compelling shared vision and that the task of leadership is to make that vision and strategy speak through facts, actions and achievements.

Such then is the incredibly complex role of a Head. And yet there are no training programmes for those aspiring to this position! Whilst there are BEd courses of hugely varying quality available throughout the country (some, I am reliably informed, are available 'over the counter'), there are no equivalents of either the IITs or the IIMs, for either training teachers or equipping them to take on the role of Heads.

More often than not, Heads are 'teachers on promotion'. Is it surprising that they tend to be confused about the expectations from their new assignment? From being expected to attain classroom objectives, to attaining institutional objectives is a huge transition—and to expect teachers to achieve this without any formal training is a big ask indeed. The fact that there are not many takers for Headship, and amongst those available, most are woefully unprepared, is therefore not surprising.

To make this depressing scenario worse, most managements are not very clear about their own roles in relation to the Head. Very often, they see the role of the Head primarily as that of ensuring quick returns on the investment made. The Head, then, is under tremendous pressure of a particular sort that takes up all the time and energy which should, otherwise, be used for purposes of real Headship.

Others see the Head as just the 'face' of the school to talk to parents and garner admissions. All the *real* decisions are taken by the owners and their families. A consequent lack of respect for the position and day-to-day interference in the running of the school, therefore, acts as another deterrent for would-be Heads, and results in a high turnover rate for the existing ones.

My own experience tells me that managements can be extremely self-centred in these matters, allowing Heads autonomy when it suits them, and withdrawing it when it does not.

In the public school that I headed where I had to deal with a support staff strike, the Board was very happy to let me deal with the strike on my own, as, if things went wrong they could find a scapegoat. Yet the same Board insisted that every case of a student being suspended had to have prior Board approval! It did not take an Einstein to figure out that members of the Board found themselves under great pressure from their friends when a student was suspended, and this was their way of protecting their backs! Managements generally fail to realize that their job is to provide a strategic view and support, act as a critical friend and ensure accountability.

If the education system is to become a powerhouse for change and provide future leadership, it must, first of all, generate excellent leaders for itself. The scenario at the moment is quite grim, forcing several schools to look at personnel from the defence services or corporate sector to step into the gap. But is that the answer? Would the army, for instance, when confronted by a serious shortage of officers, recruit its generals from the corporate sector? Certainly not, and with very good reason. True leadership must emerge, as it were, from the ranks. Only then does that leadership have the credibility and competence that it needs.

As a nation, we are duty-bound to create systems by which our young are entrusted to the care of top flight, highly trained, motivated, sensitive and caring teachers. To do this we have to ensure that bright, young and enthusiastic people join the profession, which is supported by professional training and appropriate compensation packages. This, in turn, will create a huge catchment area for future Heads. In short, we have to bring school education to the front burner.

9

Of This and That

Education in India is a subject that stretches over such a huge canvas, that it would be very difficult for any one person, leave alone someone such as myself, to even claim to be familiar with all the issues involved. I have, in the preceding pages, tried to address some of the matters of concern that I am familiar with, in the fond hope that readers may be encouraged to ponder on, discuss and debate this critical subject. There are, however, certain subtexts that very often do not get the attention they deserve, and it may be worth our while to cast our eyes on these.

One of the questions that I am frequently asked is, 'Where should I send my child? A day or boarding school?' There are, I am afraid, no easy answers to this, and all I can do is to offer my assessment of the strengths and weaknesses of these two different kinds of institutions and leave it to the reader to make the final call.

Let us first look at the boarding school scenario. This is by no means a homogenous group, and includes a broad spectrum. There are, first, the classical public schools in the mould of the Etons and Harrows of the world, to which belong our very own Doon School, Scindia School, Lawrence School, Welham Boys, Welham Girls, Mayo College and their ilk. Since most 'aspirational' upper middle-class parents have this group in mind when considering admission for their wards, it might be worth our while looking closely at this conglomerate.

These public schools are the genuine article inasmuch as that they follow all the norms laid down by the umbrella organization: The Indian Public School's Society, to which they belong. Any other school that advertises itself as 'public' is only masquerading. Among the many norms laid down for a public school by the society are: 1) It cannot be run for profit: 2) it must be totally residential; 3) it must be non-denominational and non-religious; 4) it must foster a holistic education; 5) it must have appropriate infrastructure, in addition to a host of other conditions. It thus becomes clear that this is a pretty exclusive group for which a large number of 'pretenders' do not qualify.

What are the relative strengths and weaknesses of these schools? Their strengths are many. First of all, they are almost the last bastions of a wholesome educational structure, whereby children learn not only in the classroom, but acquire a great many life skills outside it. In a situation where schools in the cities have virtually no access to open spaces, leave alone playgrounds, these schools provide the much-needed 'lungs' for their students. These schools have the great virtue of bringing together children from a variety of backgrounds, religions, castes and communities and teach them to live together without even noticing the difference. In current times, that is a singular contribution indeed.

Of course they teach self-reliance and the ability to take responsibility for one's own life. The quality of lifelong friendships that develop amongst many who attend these schools is truly amazing and to be applauded. The insistence upon complete equality (uniforms, pocket money, etc.) is a great virtue; but I am afraid is being seriously challenged by extremely ambitious and demanding parents. The fact that these schools are normally situated at a distance from the polluted city is no small advantage.

What is equally true is that these schools are facing several challenges in the context of the changing times. The first of these is of a universal nature in that it has affected the entire education sector: A serious paucity of good teachers.

The problem is vastly more accentuated in the case of public schools for a host of reasons: their geographical isolation in some cases, the inability to pay as much as the more affluent schools in the metros, the lack of access for the teachers to a tuition market, the crying shortage of men in the profession which has hit the boys' schools in particular, the inability to tap the huge pool of talented and educated ladies which the metro schools are able to do—these are some of the factors that have made the catchment area for public schools much smaller in a profession that is already thin on the ground. This naturally impacts the quality of education that they are able to deliver.

The other area of challenge is the kind of clientele that seems to be flocking to these schools. Many parents seem to choose these schools only for their 'brand value', without any real understanding of the culture these schools are trying to promote. These parents find, for instance, the restrictions on pocket money or outings and all that makes for the essential ethos of these schools, particularly galling. As a result, they place themselves in serious confrontation with the school.

This, naturally enough, has its fallout on the entire school community. This phenomenon can be seen in day schools as well, but perhaps for different reasons.

The parental attitudes are bound to impact the students as well. Whatever the sceptics may say, India is a country on the move. There are many opportunities to be had, and there is a multitude of young people anxious to grab them. NGO-run schools, Kendriya Vidyalayas and government schools are full of extremely bright and motivated students who are hungry for success.

Unfortunately, the clientele of public schools, to a large extent, comes from a section of society which, having achieved the affluence and status it desires, has lost the hunger for success. Often, these students attend the school to acquire the 'brand mark', or perpetuate the family tradition. Moreover, education tends to be viewed by both parents and students as a consumer product: 'I pay, therefore I must get'.

A combination of mediocre teachers and cynical, sometimes smug, students, who realize that if they are indeed desperate to excel in the examination, they can and must fall back on private tuitions in the vacation, does not contribute to creating a culture of learning in the school. Neither does it help create a culture of excellence. Given the kind of play fields and other sporting facilities these schools possess, should they not be producing more sporting heroes for the nation? I, for one, find it difficult to think of even one sports star that this system has thrown up.

One of the greatest banes of the public school system, and indeed one touched on earlier, is that they tend to be steeped in hierarchy. The 'senior-junior' pecking order is an integral part of the ethos of these schools and, when taken to an extreme, can result in bullying of a most horrific kind. It is well known that fear stunts growth, even if the diehards insist that 'bullying makes a man out of you'. As a corollary, what often develops in these schools is a 'herd mentality', where it takes an exceptionally brave soul to take an independent stand on any issue. Conformity becomes the norm.

An interesting observation was made to me by a young student of architecture who was researching the design of the venerable public schools. He pointed out to me that these schools were designed in a way that bred a sense of awe in their students and, more importantly, perhaps trapped them in the web of history that they represented. Which is why many 'traditions' such as bullying become entrenched in the culture of these schools. He also pointed out that the residence of the Head of school in these cases is almost always very regal and grand, located, more often than not, at a distance from the school and hemmed in by tight security. This creates an aura of inaccessibility, which is the last thing a good Head should project.

Management is yet another issue. Like the rest of the country, the management here, too, is largely in the hands of non-educationists. So while in certain parts of the sector we have liquor and property mafias managing schools, here it is mainly the 'old tie mafia'. This lack of professionalism has far-reaching implications. Public schools undoubtedly have much to recommend them. Given the all-round development of the child that they offer, they very often appear like oases in the dreary desert of education in our country. But they will seriously have to reinvent themselves to remain relevant.

These days, there is an entire plethora of boarding schools available: Ranging from the swank 'international schools' with five-star facilities and, very often, an expat Head, to the more modest establishments run by say, the Ramakrishna Mission or the Krishnamurti Foundation, the Sainik schools and a host of others. They may or may not share the characteristics of the classical public school. But the fact that they are boarding establishments produces some elements of commonality.

And the one thing I never tire of telling parents is that not every child is cut out for a boarding life. Some do thrive in it, but an equal number spend their days in misery. Five-star or not, the very fact that there are so many students of varying ages living together without parental support, is not something every child is equipped to deal with. As a parent, it behoves us to spend a lot of time, effort and energy (and indeed seek professional support if necessary) before taking that call on behalf of our progeny.

There is another issue that often gets thrown up in the public domain—and that is, when a tragedy unfortunately occurs and a child loses their life, either on account of an accident that may have been prevented by proper safety measures or, in some cases even suicide, on account of bullying or perhaps corporal punishment. TV anchors and newspaper columnists then have a field day vilifying schools and teachers. 'Experts' are summoned on television to pass pompous judgement.

Whilst the loss of a child's life is an irreparable one and deserves all the attention it can get, I do not know whether it is appropriate to vilify the entire system when such an incident occurs. After all, the army, the judiciary and the medical profession all have their share of lapses. Do we, therefore, pillory the entire organization? It would be far more meaningful perhaps, to, try and plug the systemic gaps, as it were, to ensure that the possibility of such tragedies occurring is reduced to naught.

There can be no condemnation strong enough if a child is driven to suicide either by corporal punishment or bullying. There can be no justification for either of these two evils, and to enter into a debate about it is as futile as entering into a debate on whether one should stop at a red light or not.

Having said that, why do these things happen in the first place? One of the reasons is what we have been banging on and on about—the almost complete lack of training and sensitization of our teachers. Even our much maligned cops are given some sort of sensitivity training. How many schools have the resources, time or, indeed, desire to remedy this situation? All that seems to matter is the steady addition of numbers and success in the board exam. Teachers have time only to rush through their classes and perhaps hurry off for tuitions.

Sadly, parents, instead of helping find solutions, often become part of the problem. The school gives one message to the child, the parent another. If a school bans cell phones, parents immediately plant one in the child's hands. The school insists on attendance, parents promptly turn up with false medical certificates. Parents think nothing of allowing underage children to drive, often resulting in horrific accidents. I once had a parent of a Class IX student proudly announce in my office that his son had driven him all the way from Delhi to Dehradun. I promptly asked him to take his son straight back and bring him by train!

Outside the school, the child is subjected to a barrage of confusing messages—from porn to glossy magazine ads to TV channels with varying religious content. The confusion is made worse when the parents and school speak in different languages. What will the child internalize? Add to this the pressure of getting into a decent college, and it is a daunting situation indeed.

Of course schools must train teachers on the vital issues of dealing with students in a firm but humane manner, and to be on constant vigil against bullying. But it is equally important for parents to reach out to the teachers, support them, perhaps become part of the school's training resources and, above all, speak in the same language to the child.

As for the issue of accidents occurring on account of lack of safety measures in place: Once again, the problem becomes highlighted only when a tragedy takes place. There is a big media hullabaloo for a while and then everything goes back to 'normal'. Why do these accidents occur? This is primarily on account of schools being unable or unwilling (or perhaps both), to invest in safety. After all, when you are sitting comfortably in a seller's market and parents are probably in a rush to run off to the temple to offer a prayer of thanks for the admission offered, they are hardly likely to ask the question, 'How good are your safety measures?' So, like teacher training, safety also is relegated to the back burner.

The problem is further compounded by several other factors. Most schools are genuinely strapped for cash, and the introduction of the Right to Education (RTE) Act, coupled with the government's inability to make up the promised subsidy and yet imposing fee control, seriously stretches a school's resources. Even school managements that genuinely desire to implement safety measures find themselves unequal to the task.

Both the national boards—the Indian Certificate of Secondary Education (ICSE) and the Central Board of Secondary Education (CBSE)—have drawn up elaborate manuals for school safety. But who is to ensure that these are implemented? More importantly, who is to train the school personnel in this critical area? I approached the State Disaster Management Authority several times for help in this matter, only to find the office closed on most occasions! When I did make contact, all they could do was to send a bored and listless official to give a talk accompanied by a PowerPoint presentation. Needless to say, most of the school slept through the entire event.

What is needed is a firm resolve on the part of all—governments, school managements, faculty, students and parents—to put effective safety measures in place. Funds will have to be located, even perhaps with some earmarked cess. Rigorous and sustained training programmes will have to be carried out and followed up with regular audits. Schools could, perhaps, experiment with the idea of setting up 'safety-audit' teams comprising parents (who have expertise in varying fields) to assist the school in this regard.

There are, I am afraid, no shortcuts where lives are at stake. We cannot bring back the precious children we have lost. But perhaps we can ensure that their lives did not go in vain.

A lot of time has been spent in looking at the systems that go into the making of the educational tapestry, and it is about time that we focused a little on the core of it all—the teacher. We can create all the systems that we want, but unless teachers see for themselves the great power that they have to be the change-makers, touch lives and, indeed, impact society, nothing much is going to happen.

Teachers must realize what powerful role models they can be, and that even if they positively impact the life of one child at any given point of time, it is likely to have a multiplier effect. That is why we, teachers, need to constantly introspect. The recent example of a government schoolteacher in Tamil Nadu, whose transfer evoked a storm of protest from the students, nearly caused the school to shut down and forced the authorities to revoke its decision, shows what a powerful impact a teacher can have.

When we resort to teaching the same notes year after year, when we look at the entire class as 'one size fits all', instead of as individuals with unique learning abilities, when we stop upgrading our knowledge, when we resort to slacking in the classroom so as to attract private tuition, when we are remiss about correcting assignments with rigour, when we discourage questioning minds, when we run down fellow teachers in front of our students, when we are not honest enough to admit that we do not know the answer, when we heap insult and humiliation on a child—we do immense harm to ourselves, our community and, most importantly, on our potential to nurture citizens of the future.

On the other hand, when we are infected with a sense of joy in our work, when we honestly place ourselves in the position of a 'first-learner', when we revel in our pure and unadulterated relationship with our young wards, when we genuinely lead by example and practice what we preach, when we set aside our egos and are humble enough to say, 'I do not know the answer, but am prepared to join you in finding out', only then will we be able to exercise, in the truest and purest sense, the immense power we have over these young minds. It was Leo Tolstoy who once said, 'They only die who do not live on in others'. Good teachers can write themselves into immortality.

In the days of the freedom struggle, leaders like Mahatma Gandhi and Rabindranath Tagore gave a clarion call to the entire nation to forego personal wealth, gain, prestige and status, and to join hands in the struggle to create a free India. Today, in a nation scarred and brutalized by hatred, corruption and dishonesty, the time has come for a clarion call to the youth to take on the dual responsibility of healing old wounds and rebuilding a fresh vibrant, new nation. And who is better equipped to issue that clarion call than us teachers? The responsibility lies fairly and squarely with us. We can either do that or choose to miss yet another opportunity for our 'tryst with destiny'.

10

Of Schools, Parents and Children

In our country, parents and schools seem to sustain an uneasy relationship—often bordering on a love-hate one. Parents who return euphoric after witnessing their child perform in the annual play or on the sports field often cannot get over thanking the school enough for their child's development. Yet the same parents can often turn almost violently antagonistic, and in some cases, as we have indeed seen, even take to the streets in protest. Schools, for their part, tend to work in a cloak of secrecy, and more often than not, cultivate an image of a very 'business-like' relationship with the parents.

The bottom line that seems to define this relationship is a lack of trust in each other. Why is this so? To my mind, it all begins with a great confusion that prevails over the expectations that both parties have of each other. Parents, who, for the most part, have very little understanding of their own children's strengths and weaknesses and consequently harbour unreal expectations, find themselves bitterly disappointed when the children do not do as well in school as they expected.

Little do they realize that in India, by and large, once you put your child into a school, s/he becomes just another face in a school uniform. With classroom numbers varying from forty to sixty, limited access to playing facilities and overworked and underpaid teachers, your child is hardly likely to receive the kind of individual attention required to bloom fully.

Having said that, many teachers, despite the limitations, do try and touch their pupils' lives. Instances abound when a child, needing comfort, solace or advice, will turn to a teacher rather than a parent. But when this happens, it is despite the system rather than because of it.

The situation is made even worse by the fact that there is really very little scope in our country for a dialogue between the prospective parent and the school about the expectations they have of each other. Parents are so relieved to have secured admission for their children, that they have neither the inclination nor the time to have a meaningful conversation with the school about its vision, their own expectations, the opportunities the school can offer and so on. Schools, for their part, are so busy dealing with numbers that they have no time for such niceties either. There are well-known schools in our metros which run three 'shifts' with a thousand students each! Where is the wherewithal for dialogue?

As a matter of fact, most schools do not even have a vision that they can share with the parents. They see their job as merely to get the student through the maze of examinations, culminating in the board examination. The schools that do have a vision and share it with parents, tend to be the upper-crest schools, out of reach of the ordinary folk.

Given this extremely shaky foundation to the relationship at the very outset, it is not surprising that the chasm only widens with the passage of time. The child's grades, for instance, seem to drop, they seem totally uninterested in school and, at times, instances of indiscipline are reported. The causes could be many—bullying, peer pressure, an unhappy home environment, a learning disability, sheer boredom. These are only a few possible causes; but, given the almost total absence of communication between parent and school, a proper assessment is never made, and school and parent continue to shift the blame to each other. If the problem is ever resolved, it is largely by default (passage of time for instance), and not because of any active intervention.

The other problem, of course, is that school managements do not take teachers (and sometimes even the Head) into confidence or even consultation whilst taking critical decisions. These decisions suddenly appear one fine day on the school notice board or some other such forum. Parents and students turn to the teachers and principal for an explanation, but none is forthcoming, and since they cannot go higher up in the food chain, suspicions are only heightened and the gap widens. There always seems to be a slow fuse burning.

The biggest fallout between parents and the school seems to occur after the Class X examination, when a student has to choose subject combinations for Classes XI and XII. Schools, more often than not, resort to a very simple (but to my mind, deeply flawed) formula in dealing with this issue. They pick the students with the highest marks in science and maths and offer them the much sought-after physics, chemistry, maths (PCM) combination. The students who secure average marks are offered the accounts and commerce stream and those with the poorest grades are rather condescendingly, allotted the humanities (provided that stream is offered at all in the school).

What this 'simple' formula does not take into account is that the Class X examination results, very often, do not in any way reflect the child's aptitude for a particular subject, and that there is a quantum leap in the level of academic rigour (particularly in the sciences) from Class X to Classes XI and XII. The Class X curriculum does very little to either challenge the student or test his grasp of the concepts that define a particular subject. Class X, more often than not, can be dealt with by good rote ability.

The situation is very different in Classes XI and XII, where without a strong conceptual grasp, a student will necessarily struggle. Moreover, the syllabus tends to be monstrously huge and even the so-called 'better' students have a difficult time of it. It is no surprise, therefore, that students flock to tuition teachers. The average classroom teacher has neither the time, nor, perhaps, the expertise to do justice to the subject during class hours—and certainly not to help the student with preparation for the entrance examinations to engineering and medical colleges, which seem to be the main 'drivers' of our entire system.

What I had experimented with in some of the schools that I headed, in order to resolve this problem, was to introduce an 'aptitude' test for the students applying to the various streams. This was a very scientifically designed test worked out by the senior faculty, who also consulted outside resources, if necessary. The test aimed at assessing whether the applicant would be able to cope with the demands of the subject-combination applied for, and advise the student accordingly. The marks obtained in the Class X examination were only one component of the entire decision-making process.

There was an interesting fallout of this experiment. There was a boy who had scored very high marks in the sciences in

Class X and, naturally enough, wanted to be offered the PCM stream. Our aptitude test, and all his past records, suggested that he would 'go under' with the PCM combination. He would, however, fare very well in the commerce stream. As soon as the school refused the option, the father of the boy moved the courts.

The case was heard in the Madras High Court. The court ruled in favour of the school, ruling that the school was not denying readmission (and, therefore, the right to an education) to the student. All it was doing was providing guidance regarding the best option of subjects to study, which it was ideally placed to do, in view of the extensive and in-depth records it possessed. And this brings home yet another point. If a school does its evaluation seriously, and 'tracks' a student's performance consistently, it is in a much better position to aid and advise when the time comes.

Given the fact that that the basic expectation of school education in the foreseeable future will remain the same—that it is merely a certification for the board examinations—very little is likely to change as far as the school-parent relationship is concerned. Parents will continue to view the school's job as one designed to make sure that the school helps their children secure great examination results, and schools will continue to see their job as one of delivering prescribed curriculum and encouraging children to crack the examination system with the magic wand of private tuitions. In between, if there are any issues affecting either this process or the safety and security of the child, or—heaven forbid—a fee hike, a dialogue, albeit of a very confrontational kind, will begin between the school and the parent.

Surely, this is not a healthy state of affairs, and the worst sufferers, as in the case of an uneasy marriage, are the children. Something surely needs to be done, given the gravity of the issue?

And in many small ways, much can be done. To start with, parents could get to know their child a bit better. It never ceases to amaze me how many parents, when confronted with something their child has done (either good or bad) respond with, 'I did not know that my son/daughter could have done this!' This response is par for the course, whether they are seeing their child's artwork for the first time, or being told that the child has been caught smoking!

One of the things I attempted to do to bridge this gap was to have the students do 'workshops' for parents. I remember one powerful presentation where the students openly discussed the impact of porn on their lives. One of the parents was utterly shocked that her son was even aware of sex, leave alone in its ugly avatar!

It is my opinion that if schools could help organize more structured interactions between parents and students, a great deal can be achieved to help them understand and empathize with each other. These interactions, because they are held on a 'neutral' venue and have many participants rather than a one-on-one situation, seem to give much more confidence to both the parties involved to have a frank discussion.

However, under no circumstances should parents (as they sadly seem wont to do) run down teachers in the presence of their children. Teachers receive very little respect in this country to begin with, without having the parents join in as well.

If parents have a genuine understanding of their children's strengths, weaknesses, aims and aspirations, such interactions could provide a solid platform for discussions with the school on a variety of subjects, including academic performance. Parents would begin to understand that not every child is cut out to be a top-of-the-line engineer, doctor or, perhaps, Test cricketer!

Schools, for their part, must be prepared to invest the time and effort required for an ongoing conversation with their students and parents. As things stand, managements, in an effort to cut costs, so overload their teachers that they have neither the time nor the energy to look at anything other than a student's classroom performance.

In most schools, there is a standard formula for allotting workloads to teachers—X number of teaching classes, X number of co-curricular responsibilities, X number of examination duties and so on. When displayed on the notice board, all of this looks very scientific and equitable.

What it does not show is that every teacher has the added responsibility of commuting to school (a nightmare in India at the best of times) and, in the case of a female teacher in our deeply patriarchal society, tending to the entire family's needs, which includes supervising the studies of one's own children. The fact that they turn up at school at all, is a bit of a miracle! And on top of all this they have to cart home volumes of assignments to evaluate!

Managements, if genuinely interested in delivering an 'education', will have to find ways and means by which teachers will have 'quality time' to spend with their students. And this will include recruiting more faculty, sensitizing and training them, and cutting down on the unmanageable numbers of students who are packed into classrooms.

The quality of interaction between parents and the school at the usual Parents-Teachers Association (PTA) meets also leaves a lot to be desired. At present, on most of these occasions, parents queue up in front of a classroom to meet their child's teacher. They are usually nervous and fidgety and anxious to get away. The teacher has a register kept open with all the grades duly entered. The discussion, on account of constraints of time and numbers, is necessarily brief and neither side has come to grips with any substantive issues, when it is over.

Schools, after having provided more quality time to their teachers, must train and sensitize their teachers to make discussions with parents broader and more meaningful. There must also be regular 'follow-up' on cases that need intervention.

At a school in the USA where I worked, the week would begin with what was called a 'retention meeting' that was attended by not only teachers but also counsellors and pastoral support staff. The faculty would go through, with a fine-tooth comb, all the appropriate records of students facing trouble in coping—emotionally, academically, socially or other issues—and strategies would be worked out to help.

In the hurly-burly of the Indian education scenario, this seems an unattainable dream, but it is definitely worth making a beginning, however humble and small.

Schools will often have to walk that extra hard mile. In a day school that I headed for a while, the faculty was completely at a loss to explain the consistently aberrant behaviour of one of the students. We then had one of the teachers 'tail' the student when he boarded the school bus to go home. The teacher followed him all the way to the apartment and saw the boy let himself in with a key hidden nearby, as both parents were away at work. And the next thing the boy did was to switch on the computer and settle down to a feast of porn! The parents were summoned and of course they were in a state of shock. The solution found was to have the boy go straight to his grandparents, and they would take him home only after the parents had returned.

PTAs could become active, vibrant bodies instead of just raising administrative issues. Parents usually represent a vast range of expertise and experience and, thus, could be invited at regular intervals to share their experiences with the students. Some schools have a 'roster' of parents willing to step in for 'substitute duty' to fill in for an absent teacher. Others rope in parents who are general physicians, dentists or eye doctors to take part in medical 'camps' for teachers and students. There are some, where parents take students out on climbing, trekking or nature trips. The opportunities are immense, and all it needs is a bit of imagination and a proactive approach from both parents and school.

All this must be backed up by a sustained dialogue between the school and parents. It is not good enough for schools to trot out their achievements in a report on the Annual Day. Schools must also regularly share with parents their failures as well, as also plans (long- and short-term), and seek help where necessary. Schools and parents must learn to embrace each other in a warm and trusting relationship. Only then will the child blossom.

What most teachers and parents find very challenging is dealing with teenagers. I am no psychologist to be able to explain the complex changes that children go through in their teens. My understanding of this phase of their lives is based solely on my experience with this age group for over three decades. That this is a very difficult time of their lives is beyond doubt. They are trying to cut off their moorings from the cocoon of family and take a shortcut to adulthood.

But, along the way they are making the painful discovery that there are in fact, no such shortcuts, and that the path is often a lonely and difficult one. In my view, the best thing that parents and teachers can do at this critical time is to be patient and supportive and, at the same time, fair and firm. We adults will, of course, have to reach out to them when they stumble, but at the same time we should not lower our expectations of them. Teenagers must realize that whilst adults will be patient and supportive, there is a very clear line that they (the teenagers) cannot cross, and crossing it will have consequences.

I recall having to deal with a particularly rebellious young man (the son of a famous film star), who had been put in boarding school for his last two years of school, much against his wishes. At most times he found the routine and restrictions of boarding school unbearable, but as he had been party to the understanding when admitted, I would brook no compromise. My interactions with him ranged from serious reprimand to answering questions like, 'What is a man of your qualification doing in a sh*** place like this?'

On the day that he was leaving, I asked him about how he felt about the experience. 'I can't say I enjoyed it, but by Jove, I will not forget it!' was the reply.

Romance between teenagers can also be a huge challenge

for the school and parents, especially in India, where there is often a great conflict of values on this subject. I have already dwelt at length in an earlier chapter on the role of the school in sensitizing students on issues surrounding relationships with the opposite sex. A school's efforts will, however, come to naught unless backed effectively by understanding, support and appreciation by parents at home.

We, as adults, often find it difficult to empathize with the confusion that young people feel on this issue. Along with a barrage of sex, romance, titillation through advertisements, Bollywood, and all that is available on the Internet, teenagers are ironically often subject to the most Victorian codes both at home and at school. And, instead of helping to sort out this terrible confusion, we tend to take judgemental stands.

My own experience tells me that while pointing out the minefields that lie in the path of those who get carried away by the tidal gulf that often accompanies teenage romance, it is best to steer them firmly but gently in the right direction.

At a co-ed boarding school that I headed, many of the faculty and parents were considerably agitated by the sight of 'couples' walking along the path in front of the 'tuck shop' (commonly known as 'lovers' lane'), gazing fondly into each other's eyes and surreptitiously holding hands. There was one ground rule that I made clear to all at the very beginning. No one, not even a teacher, was allowed to chastize any such behaviour in public. If ever there was a case of an excessive display of affection the faculty member either dealt with it in the privacy of a study, or reported it to me. I never faced the same problem from the same source a second time.

As much as my heart went out to the young lovebirds,

I had to perforce do something. I, thereupon, summoned the representatives of the student body and had a frank and free discussion on the matter. The result was an ingenious solution: The decrepit tuck shop was moved to more congenial surroundings, given a facelift and an 'official dating time' was declared on Sundays when the budding Romeos and Juliets could meet in civilized, cheerful, safe and undisturbed surroundings, even if only to whisper 'sweet nothings' to each other! Peace reigned.

A similar situation prevailed with regard to the 'socials' or 'dances' as they were called. The practice, when I joined, was to have a termly dance to which the entire middle and senior school were invited. I was quite horrified when I saw my first 'social'. The boys and girls assembled in a large hall with the two sexes huddled at either end, casting nervous glances at each other. The scene was quite akin to that portrayed in that famous film, *The Dirty Dozen*, in which the twelve men being sent off on a suicide mission during the war are 'entertained' on the last night by a truckload of women carted in from the town! Teachers, armed with torches, patrolled the premises in order to prevent anything untoward from happening especially if the lights went out briefly, as they often seemed to do. I seethed in disgust.

Once again, prolonged discussions were entered into with the student body. The upshot was that several ground rules were laid down by the students themselves. They agreed to dress appropriately for the evening, spend time in actually conversing with each other (rather than ogling) and then my wife, Indrani, and I would lead off by taking the floor for the first dance—Indrani with the head boy and I with the head girl. Thereafter, the young Galahads would approach their partners and the evening was on! It was amazing how much a simple conversation with the students, based on respect and understanding for each other, could achieve!

The senior students then, in fact, took the business of 'socials' to a different level altogether. Inspired, perhaps, by my colleagues and I constantly reminding them of the need to develop relationships based on mutual respect, they came up with the idea of a 'termly dinner'. On the appointed evening, the senior boys would dress up in their Sunday best, walk up to the Girls' School and escort their partners (dressed equally well) for a formal dinner. After dinner, considerable time was given for relaxed conversation with light music in the background and then, at an agreed hour, the boys would escort the ladies back to their hostel. It is a matter of some pride for me that never once during my nine-year stint at the school, was I ever let down on this score.

That was in late 1990s. Contrast this with what happened in a school in Kerala in December 2017. I reproduce below my Facebook post on the subject:

> Last night, I watched in horror a TV debate on NDTV 24×7. From this debate, I learned the following:
>
> A 'leading' school in a 'leading' (at least in terms of numeracy and education) state of our country, suspended a class XII boy from the school some 5 months back for hugging a friend (a girl) on the school campus, in public view, for what the school considered an inordinate length of time. Needless to say, the school considered this an 'immoral' act, and is also considering the possibility of

banning the young man from appearing for his board examinations later in the academic year. Incidentally, the young lady in question says that she had no objection to being hugged by a friend. One thing was clear from all parties—this was just a hug, pure and simple.

The father of the boy has taken the matter to the courts for resolution. The principal of this 'leading' school says that though the boy has apologized for his actions, he is to be blamed for the pictures of this event having gone viral on social media. And this is a principal who lives and works in this era of technology!

A supposedly 'leading' educationist of the country was one of the panelists on the debate. Apart from some wishy-washy arguments where it was clear that she did not want to take a stand, she, in fact, offered a rather weak and obtuse defence of the school's stance!

If this is where our education system is heading and that too in one of our more progressive states, then all I can say is, 'Cry, the Beloved Country!'

We need to seriously engage with our young folk on these issues, if we have to help bring them up to have genuine respect for each other, irrespective of gender or other differences.

Substance abuse is yet another 'area of darkness' that schools and parents are haunted by. Whilst not being a great authority on the subject, I can only share what worked for me. The last assignment that I had as Head of school before I retired, was to head a boarding school for boys, whose reputation at the time was at an all-time low, particularly because of a frightening upsurge in the incidence of substance abuse. As a matter of fact, a recent alumnus of the school had been stabbed to death in the university he had just joined on account of a gang war over drugs.

I quickly realized that the problem was so widespread that it could not be treated as a 'law and order' problem, but as a 'community' one. The first thing I did, as the new Head, was to write to all the parents admitting that we had a huge problem on our hands and that they could exercise either of the two options—withdraw their son from the school or join us in the 'crusade' that we were about to launch. Some, however small a number, took the first option but most decided to give the second one a shot. The next step was to bring up this issue at a wider meeting of local Heads of schools in order to see how they were coping and learn something from them. To my surprise, almost al the schools went into denial: 'We have no such problem here,' was the common refrain.

So it was clear that we would have to do it on our own. Sometimes, however, help comes from the most unexpected quarters. A local NGO, which worked towards the rehabilitation of addicts, came to my rescue. They organized a series of seminars, workshops and talks by former addicts on this issue. The senior students participated enthusiastically as they were seeing some of their closest friends going down the slippery path.

In what was one of the most trying moments of my career, ten students were identified as hard core users and the Board decided to make an example of them and ordered their expulsion from the school. I had sleepless nights on the issue and appealed to the Chairman to give me one more chance with these young men. To his credit, and my eternal gratitude, he acceded to my request.

To cut a long story short, these ten young 'leaders' became the spearhead for the anti-substance abuse programme in the school. They made a powerful feature film on the subject, with themselves in the lead roles, and this had a huge impact on all. They addressed the school openly and honestly, and shared all their experiences, however ghastly.

Help came from another unexpected quarter. The Director General of Police, Aloke Lal, who was equally concerned about this scourge, volunteered to help. Not only did he do workshops with the students, he also enlisted the help of his force to act as 'decoys' and flush out suppliers. Soon, word got around that the school was not to be messed around with. Parents were invited to join in both as participants and active advisers.

It was now a question of time before the entire school took a solemn vow, that never again would they allow themselves to plunge down this precipice. And I can proudly say that during the remainder of my stint there, they were as good as their word.

What are schools for? To bring up, I think, right-thinking young adults who will be productive, effective and caring members of society. Parents, schools, teachers, principals, management, students and, indeed, the local community have to see themselves as part of an organic whole and be involved in this effort. The power that can emanate from a synergy of all these energies and efforts can be truly transformative. In the immortal words of John Lennon:

You may say I'm a dreamer
But I'm not the only one
I hope some day you'll join us
And the world will be as one.

11

The Lighter Side

As any schoolteacher will testify, in dealing with students, almost each day brings a new surprise. That is what makes our profession so much fun, and so different from all others.

The following anecdotes are by no means comprehensive and nor are they intended to convey any deep meaning or lesson. They are just what they were then, and will always remain—a whole load of fun and learning.

I started my career in the Doon School in 1983. The Doon School, as is well-known, is a hoary establishment replete with traditions and practices. Many of these were, of course, devised by the boys themselves, and often set up as a challenge for succeeding generations to do 'better' (in a manner of speaking). One such challenge was the business of 'bunking' (or breaking bounds) from school and ordering a veritable feast from one of the local eateries in order to impress and entertain one's friends—a completely illegal act, of course, in terms of school rules. But, the bigger the feast, the better.

On one such occasion, a young man was moved by his mates to seriously take on the challenge. He, thereupon, planned to slip out at games-time, go to one of the better-known culinary establishments dotting the famous 'Suicide Alley' and order the schoolboys' dream—plates of 'butter chicken'. (It never ceases to amaze me how many generations of Doon valley students revere this as an iconic dish, along with another mysterious item that revels in the name of 'bun-samosa'.) The order also included biryani, kebabs and hot 'naans'. It was a feast fit for kings and the young man was quite looking forward to carving his name in immortality.

The plan was carefully laid. Dressed in casuals, the lad skipped across the boundary wall, went up to the eatery, and placed his order. Directions were given carefully about the delivery point: a gaping hole in the wall not far from 'Jaipur House' gate. The proprietor fondly caressed the wad of notes handed over to him.

However, as the old saying goes 'the best-laid plans of mice and men often go awry'. It so happened that the 'delivery boy' on the day was a new hand, not quite familiar with the geography of the school. Nodding confidently in deference to his employers wishes, he set off for his mission.

Alas, at the school he found himself thoroughly confused by the gates, and started panicking on seeing the security guards. Rather than inviting any trouble (he had heard about the reputation of the school), he quickly put down his precious cargo in front of the Headmaster's gate and fled!

The security guards, not quite sure whether this was a bomb planted by terrorists, quickly grabbed the huge package (those were the days before the advent of sophisticated security devices) and delivered the caboodle straight to the then Headmaster, Shomie Das!

Shomie, an old hand at the trade himself (he was an ex-student of the school), quickly sized up the situation and spotted a huge opportunity. Phone calls went out to all of us housemasters to summon us for an 'emergency' meeting. And over some fine whiskey and undoubtedly great food, we humble housemasters were treated to one of the finest evenings of our lives in the school!

∽

To continue with the theme of 'bunking'. It was not only food that was the driving force for a 'bunk'. There were some intrepid souls who took the plunge in order to catch a late-night movie—more for the thrill, than the film, I suppose.

On one such occasion, the young man happened to have a rather formidable housemaster who was popularly known as 'AD'. AD was a bit of a legend in the school, the reputation fuelled by his extraordinary love and attachment for the boys, coupled with the propensity to indulge in what could appear to be extraordinarily eccentric behaviour.

On that particular night, AD was on his rounds of the house, when he noticed a rather carefully crumpled up bed designed to look as if the occupant was asleep under the covers. Of course the occupant was away in some film theatre in town. AD carefully crawled under the covers. Way past midnight, the young lad made his way back, congratulating himself on having pulled off a great dare and even treated himself to a congratulatory ' bun-samosa' at 'Jattis'—the nearest eatery. He then slipped into his pyjamas and, bleary-eyed, crawled into bed, only to find himself in the warm embrace of a rather bemused, and I daresay, sleepy housemaster! What would I not have given for that 'Woody Allen' moment to see the look on their faces!

On one bitterly cold Dehradun winter night, I had been

invited to dinner at a friend's home. Indrani opted out to babysit our children. My vehicle at that point of time was a rather noisy 'Yezdi 'motorcycle, a model rather a rage in those days, and was well known to the boys. However, on that particular night, my trusted steed let me down, and I had to perforce borrow a Vespa scooter from a colleague. To protect myself from the cold I had donned my frayed old parka from my college days.

As I was driving back from the dinner, rather late at night, I noticed a figure thumbing a ride by the roadside. I recognized him as 'VK', a student from Jaipur House. With my face partially covered by my parka's hood, VK, of course, had no way of recognizing me.

'*Bhai sahab, mujhe Doon School tak chod denge*? (Sir, would you be kind enough to drop me off at the Doon School?)' he asked, and to make things easier for a stranger, he added: '*Main gate tak* (up to the main gate)'.

I grunted a reply and we set off. As it happened, the Jaipur House gate was located a little before one got to the main gate. I stopped at the gate, whipped my hoodie off and remarked rather grandly, 'Mr VK, I rather think that is where you want to get off!'

VK turned pale, stuttered something and, in the process, nearly fell off the scooter. With a cheerful 'See you tomorrow' (much in the nature of 'Heigh-ho, Silver Away'), I drove off. We met the next day in the Housemaster's study, and after delivering a suitable admonishment, the housemaster and I keeled over with laughter!

Interaction with students tends to be a bit different once one is the Head of the school. But there are huge opportunities nonetheless and a great deal depends on the Head's personality and how he responds. There are occasions when a Head can find himself torn between the child in him and the need to be seen as a figure of authority.

In the Lawrence School, Ooty, which was my first Headship, there was a brilliant but rather irascible maths teacher. Whilst the students respected him for his teaching abilities, they often found themselves at the wrong end of his temper. I had been made aware that plans were afoot to deal with the situation, and I hoped desperately that nothing really unpleasant would happen.

One day, the opportunity for the students arose. The teacher was taking a class just below theirs. Through the tiny gaps in the wooden planks that constituted the floor, the plotters could catch glimpses of their bête noir's sparsely populated top. They, therefore, poured an entire bottle of ink through the cracks right on the unsuspecting head!

The teacher was furious. Not being able to identify the culprit, he marched up the entire class straight to my office, demanding strict disciplinary action. I was completely nonplussed. One part of me screamed with laughter and wanted to say, 'well done!', and yet I was acutely aware that I could not let the faculty down. Of course, serious admonishments were administered—the entire class suffered temporary loss of privileges, and had to offer a public apology at assembly the next day. Whew!

Occasionally, perhaps rarely, is the Head presented with an opportunity such as the one I am about to describe. I had just assumed my first Headship—of the Lawrence school, which stretched over miles of forest land that teemed with wildlife, particularly boars that constantly marauded nearby crops and our own school gardens. Those were the days when wildlife laws were not so stringent and, in fact, boars were considered vermin. I had enjoyed the odd boar shoot in my previous town—Dehradun—and was not yet saddled with pacemakers and defibrillators. (Ironically, much later in my stint at this school, I was persecuted endlessly for supposedly having shot a boar, at a time when I was packed with pacemakers and defibs, and could hardly have picked up a gun, leave alone fire one!)

But to cut back to the story—the school's director of physical education (a rather military-like Coorgi gentleman, known to share his kinsfolk's appetite for, what in the parlance was known as, 'wine and swine'), invited me for an evening out to secure ourselves some of this delicacy. He also guaranteed that that we would not have very far to go and neither would we be disappointed. I was quite relieved as the Nilgiris can get very wet, cold and blustery in August.

As it turned out, my intrepid companion took me to a huge tree just behind what were called the 'big-bogs' (this was a cavernous dungeon-like structure that housed the toilets for the senior boys) and was reputedly the 'hang-out' for those who desired a 'smoke' or a wee 'shot' to ward off the cold. I must confess that I was not privy to all these nuggets yet, as I had been in school only for a week and the students had just returned from their break the evening before.

The tree in question overlooked a potato patch on the hill

side, and my enterprising friend had rigged up a make-shift machan on one of the overhanging branches. Armed with a flask of coffee (and, of course, a shotgun) and protected by my trusted parka and 'hoodie', I was all set for some excitement.

We did not have to wait for long. A troop of boar proceeded up the hill, chomping noisily. Visions of a nice roast and perhaps some achar, heightened the anticipation. Alas! Just as the beasts were within range, loud raucous laughter and cheering erupted in the 'big-bog'. The seniors were having a celebration! The boar vanished in seconds. I could see smoke wafting out of the windows and could also smell alcohol.

Furious, mainly at being robbed of some great gastronomical delights, I jumped off the tree, carrying my shotgun, with my partner in close pursuit. I jumped into the dungeon through one of the open windows. The boys had no idea who this apparition was, least of all that it was their new Head of school. They gazed in awe and fright as the hooded figure waved the gun in their direction, with the order 'hands up!'

Cigarette butts showered down on the floor and there was sound of glass tumblers shattering.

'To the Headmaster's office,' I barked and marched the lot up. There was even more consternation when the hooded figure sat himself down on the Head's chair, whipped out a notebook and proceeded to write down the coordinates of all 'arrested', with the accompanying introduction: 'Gentleman, I am the new Headmaster!'

The matter was satisfactorily resolved the next day by the timely intervention of the housemasters who promised assurances for the future conduct of their wards, and we proceeded with the new term, albeit on a note that I had not expected!

∽

Then there are occasions, which, so to speak, fall into your lap and you have a chance to either form bonds or make an impact. Being a passionate runner, the verdant forests of the Lawrence School afforded me some great opportunities to indulge in my passion. Whenever possible, I always used to encourage some of the boys to accompany me on these runs.

The campus being spread over seven hundred acres of forest also provided sanctum to many local bootleggers for brewing their lethal wares. Once, when out on a run with some of the boys, we came across one such bivouac. The bootlegger obviously took to his heels. Little did he know that this crazy Headmaster and his gang in hot pursuit were fully equal to the task. The chase was over three miles of hill and dale, but we finally apprehended the culprit and handed him over to the local constabulary. I am not entirely sure, but I do recall feeling that some of the senior boys looked at me with a new-found respect from that day onwards.

∽

Not all interactions, however, are always pleasant, and, at times, split-second decisions have to be taken, giving considerable room later for regret perhaps? At my last school, as I have described earlier, there was a serious problem of substance abuse. One of the measures we had to take, much to my dislike, was to organize surprise 'inspections' of personal belongings and nearby spaces to hunt for contraband.

During one such 'inspection' that I was observing from close quarters, I noticed one of the young men start to stiffen noticeably as his housemaster approached. Something about the boy's body language told me that trouble was brewing and so I quickly sidled closer. When the boy was asked to open his case, he refused. An argument started to develop and I was startled at the speed with which the issue snowballed.

Suddenly, I guessed by the look on the boy's face and his clenched fist, that he was about to hit his teacher. There was no time to do anything else, other than to jump in, yank the young man by the collar, virtually hoist him on to my shoulder, and deposit him at a safe distance. And all this while the rest of the house was watching!

I agonized a great deal later about whether I could have handled the situation differently. Till this day, I have not found an answer. However, mercifully, after the dust settled, I had the opportunity to talk things calmly over with the boy and, indeed, his father, and whilst I have no way of being absolutely certain, I do think that the matter was resolved amicably. At any rate, I did not have any further trouble from that quarter.

There are occasions when one's colleagues make the ground shift from under one's feet, by say, accepting lavish gifts from parents. They, thereby, put themselves and the school in a compromising position especially when the student concerned commits a misdemeanour. It is very difficult, and often churlish, to refuse a gift, especially when it is meant as a genuine mark of gratitude. The best judge of that is the recipient of the gift himself and they have to take the call as to whether refusal is going to hurt feelings, or acceptance is going to lead to further compromise. In any case, one thumb rule as far as I am concerned: Never accept a gift which you cannot afford to buy for yourself, or cannot repay in monetary value.

Our profession is a hugely exciting and, often, an unpredictable one. Every day brings with it a new experience, new learning, a chance to do something different, or differently, and to reach out and touch lives. A teacher who looks upon each day with anticipation and excitement is more likely to bring joy and satisfaction to his work and, therefore, in the lives of others. As the old phrase goes, 'Carpe Diem' (seize the moment)!

12

Reflections of a Teacher

In March 2009, I had an unexpected visitor at Welham Boys' School, Dehradun. Joseph Loftin, the Head of a prestigious private boarding school in the USA—the Wasatch Academy—was on a visit to India, prospecting for schools to partner with. Joe and I struck up an immediate rapport as we found a huge amount of common ground in our views on education. Our schools did enter into a very productive partnership, but what is of relevance here is that Joe attended one of my school assemblies where I would, as a matter of routine, address the student body. As we walked out of that particular assembly, Joe said to me, 'I must have you deliver the keynote address at our graduation day ceremony this year.'

I thought that it was just a casual conversational remark, and so was very surprised when, a few weeks after Joe's departure, I received a return ticket to Salt Lake City, Utah, the airport nearest to the school. Thus it was in the May of that year, I found myself addressing a congregation of parents, faculty and students at the Wasatch Academy. The speech seemed to have been fairly well-received, as I was approached by large groups from the audience afterwards, full of questions, particularly about education and India. Joe, as a matter of fact, wrote to my Board saying that was the finest graduation speech the school had in its entire history! It was also the prime reason, I suspect, for Wasatch Academy to offer my wife and me jobs, as soon as I retired from Welham in 2011, which, as it turned out, proved to be a life-changing experience.

The graduation ceremony itself was an extremely revealing experience. In India, we do have farewells for the outgoing classes, but the pomp and ceremony with which the Americans say farewell to their graduating students is on a different level altogether.

I must confess at the very outset that, as I stood there before the assembly, I found myself a trifle bemused. Bemused at the fact that a little-known Head teacher such as myself should be invited to come all the way from India to address such an august audience in the United States of America. It was, to begin with, a truly humbling experience and one for which I felt immensely grateful as well as privileged.

Two days prior to the ceremony (I had reached a few days early so that I could get a feel of the place before writing and delivering my speech), a few students came to visit me to have an informal chat. Upon discovering my interest in horses, they immediately decided to give me a taste of the ultimate American—or Western—experience of a genuine 'rodeo'. The school had a very active riding programme, and the riders were happy to showcase their skills. I was very grateful for the rodeo that was put up in my honour. Not only was it an awesome experience, it also gave me an idea about what I could do, perhaps, with my more difficult students—I would just send them across to be put on one of those bulls!

On a more serious note, however, this invite to Wasatch also told me something about the academy and the man who headed it. How many Heads of schools, anywhere in the world, would have the courage to invite a totally unknown quality from halfway across the globe, on the basis of just one meeting in faraway India?

It said a great deal about the man who made the decision, and something about the institution that he was trying to create. It told me that here was a school with a bold leader, a man gifted with a global vision. In my experience of education, most schools are managed rather than led. Wasatch was truly fortunate inasmuch as it was not only very well managed, but was also brilliantly led.

And that impression was only strengthened by my few days on campus. The incredible diversity I had seen there—the school had students from thirty-eight different nationalities—the openness and warmth of the place, the commitment and feeling of ownership evident amongst all there convinced me that what Wasatch was engaged in was an experiment of universal significance—an experiment that symbolized the effort of this wonderful institution to put together a brave new world. And it was my fond hope that my school would be able to draw strength and inspiration from the relationship that we hoped to forge in the days to come.

As I stood there before the audience at the graduation, my mind went back to my own graduation at high school. It was a relatively small affair, with only us students and our teachers in attendance, but the Principal had taken the trouble to invite a guest speaker on the occasion. The worthy gentleman urged us to gird our loins in preparation for the struggle that lay ahead of us. He warned us against the dangers that lay in wait for us in the 'big bad world' outside school, and how we should be ready to take the battle to the enemy. I sat there aghast, my young mind reeling under this onslaught. Here I was, on the threshold of adulthood, looking forward to a whole world of warm, human relationships. But here I was being exhorted to sharpen my sword and plunge it into the chest of whosoever dared to cross my path! And the crowning glory of the speech was when the speaker ended with the thumping homily, 'Remember boys, God helps those who help themselves!'

'Hey,' I remember saying to myself, 'from what I know of God, he should be the guy who helps those who **can't** help themselves!'

When I decided to become a teacher, I was convinced that I, for one, would never go down that road with my students. As an educator, I felt that my task was to excite them about the future, and to inspire them to take on the challenge of making the world a better place.

As adults, however, we would be fools not to tell our students of the challenges they face. Our generation has, unfortunately, bequeathed to them a world that is hurtling towards an era of inequity and social injustice.

Once I had assumed my responsibilities at Wasatch a few years later, I could not help but be acutely dismayed by the culture of 'waste', particularly when it came to food, that prevailed in the US. I would point out to my American students that in 1900, when an average American went to the market, he had a choice of three hundred items to buy in a market space of 150 square metres. In 2000, when an American living in a city with a population of 100,000 went to a market, he had a choice of one million items in a market space of 1.5

million square metres. Yet in 2008, there were forty million people living in poverty in the US—that is one in nearly seven Americans. And, over fourteen million children, that is, 19 per cent of the total children in this country, were living below the poverty line.

I would also point out (as indeed I used to do to my students in India), that in our own country, after sixty-five years of independence, 70 per cent of the people lived in poverty, 50 per cent of the children were malnourished, and we housed 50 per cent of the world's illiterate. In a population of a 1,120 million people, there was no electricity in the homes of 800 million (of course, that situation has been largely rectified today). Between 1998 and 2003, approximately 100,000 farmers committed suicide mainly owing to debt. Yet the numbers of billionaires had gone up from nine in 2003 to forty in 2007.

We are also being recognized as an emerging IT superpower, with our professionals manning the most sensitive positions in this field across the globe. We pride ourselves on being a member of the prestigious 'Nuclear club' of nations. Our politicians and economists boastfully claimed that the worldwide recession has not singed us. Does recession really matter to people who do not have anything to start with anyway? As the old saying goes: 'What's money when you don't have any?' Little did (Bob) Dylan know when he wrote those immortal lyrics that how much the times they would be 'a-changin'!

It is often all too easy to bombard people with statistics, but these truly make sense only when related with a very personal, life-changing experience. So I did seize the opportunity to tell my young American friends about a life-changing experience that I had experienced. I was also very acutely aware, as I related this incident, that I ran the risk of reinforcing stereotypes about India. I, therefore, cautioned my students not to take that view. India is far too complex a country, I advised, to be reduced to a stereotype.

In 2007, I was on my way to a tiger reserve—Jim Corbett National Park—which was located a few hours' drive away from my school. The tiger, I informed them, is an endangered species and only about a thousand of them (at the time), survived in such parks. (Incidentally, Wasatch's mascot was a tiger, and during my stay there I had the opportunity to bring out a group of students to study the relationship between the environment and the tiger in Madhya Pradesh.)

On the way to Corbett, I had stopped for a while at a friend's farm located at the edge of the Park. My friend took me for a short walk into the forest where there was a small settlement of a nomadic and pastoral people called the 'Gujars'. The Gujars have an interesting lifestyle. They raise buffaloes and, in the summer months, the men-folk go up to the grazing pastures in the mountains, leaving the women and children in the settlement to care for the old and ailing livestock.

I was not quite prepared for what I saw. There were about eight or ten women and a dozen odd children living in the most primitive of conditions. There was no electricity or water supply, and no provision for any medical care and, of course, education. The children had to fetch water from a point about three miles away, after negotiating forests full of wild animals. The head of the settlement was an old woman who revelled in the name of 'Akal bai', which loosely translated to 'Wise lady'.

I asked Akal bai what it was that I could fetch for her from the city. She said, 'Son, it would be wonderful if you could get me a torch. We have a big problem with wild elephants at night and I might be able to scare them off with a torch!'

As I was speaking to her there was an almighty commotion and a buffalo came charging into the settlement. Half of her back had been badly torn up by a tiger and she had barely managed to get away! As there were no medicines available, my friend and I drove into the nearest town an got hold of the necessary medicines with which we patched up the poor animal. I am glad to report that it survived!

Later that night I stood in the forest and held out my palms in front of me. It was so dark that I could not see anything. I thought of those Gujar children who live like this night after night, surrounded by wild animals. And this was twenty-first century India, proudly claiming to be an emerging 'Superpower'! 'What right do I have,' I thought to myself, 'to complain, I, who for no reason other than an accident of birth, found myself privileged enough to hog the precious resources of this earth, whilst these little children, for no fault of their own, were condemned to the life they led. What justice is this?' I told my young American students that I was still searching for that answer, albeit without success. Perhaps their generation would find it.

The argument I was making was not against progress, but against the kind of progress that creates such an inequitable and unjust social order. It is the kind of process that makes a mockery of the fundamental values of a democracy and robs the political process of any kind of credibility. Today, when a political leader expresses his concern for the underprivileged, is it surprising that no one is fooled?

And what does such a skewed pattern of development, I went on to point out, does to the environment? We have, as noted environmentalists have repeatedly pointed out, blindly followed a development paradigm inherited from the Reductionist legacy of observing natural processes in their isolation, detached from the vast interconnection of things. Such a paradigm, they have indicated, creates great ecological and economic instability.

Thus, we have chemical agriculture, which no doubt enhances productivity, but has devastating side-effects. We see antibodies as a magical cure but forget that this dependence gives rise to newer kinds of resistant drugs and diseases. In India, in a slavish imitation of the West and even Japan, we have released millions of automobiles without the supporting infrastructure of roads, parking spaces. Anyone who lives in a major Indian city today, as doubtless their Head of school who had visited India would tell them, deserves a bravery award! You have a rodeo in your equestrian centre here, I pointed out. But we have one on every street! In fact, it seems we are riding a bull most of the time!

Furthermore, genetic engineering, the damming of interlinking rivers, etc., have all brought with them an attendant chain of horrors. The consumption patterns we have released spell disaster for the future. The Centre for Science and Environment in India had calculated that the country's Environmental Degradation Cost (EDP) is 7–9 per cent of its Gross Domestic Product (GDP)!

India generates roughly 38,000 million litres of sewage daily. Even for the record the government has the capacity to deal with only 12,000 million litres—that is less than one one-third of the muck. In the US, an average American creates 56 tonnes of waste every year, to remove which requires 63,000 waste dumpers. New York City alone generates 24,000 tonnes of municipal waste every day. Talk about dumping your problems on the next generation!

Somewhere along the line, I am convinced that we have lost that fine balance between man and nature—a balance that, centuries ago, the Buddha saw as necessary for the survival of the human race, when he exhorted mankind to follow the 'middle path' between extreme asceticism and extreme self-indulgence.

These are dangerous portends that need to be addressed. Otherwise, I imagine a world where the 'wretched of the earth', as Frantz Fanon called them, turn around to the rich, and to paraphrase Shylock in *The Merchant of Venice,* say, 'Hath not the poor eyes? Hath not the poor hands, organs, senses, dimensions, affections, passions? If you prick us do we not bleed? If you tickle us do we not laugh? If you poison us do we not die? *And if you wrong us shall we not revenge?*' And let me assure you, as we are indeed finding out in pockets of our own country, 'Hell hath no fury like the dispossessed scorned.'

I am aware that I may sound like a prophet of gloom, but that is certainly not what I envision for the future. On the contrary, I see a future full of hope wherever in the world I meet students and look into the eyes of these confident young faces around me. Theirs is a generation which is far ahead of ours in many ways. To begin with, they have access to much more information than we ever had. Information, when processed correctly, will lead to knowledge, and knowledge, when tempered with experience, and even suffering, will lead to wisdom.

They also have a degree of self-confidence and optimism which very few of us dared to have. They have the courage to take risks, they carry less baggage in terms of old memories, prejudices, biases and animosities. They know no geographical frontiers. They have many more avenues to express their creativity, to attain self-realization. I am convinced that we are bequeathing this world to a far better, and an infinitely more competent, pair of hands.

So if I may dare (at the risk of sounding terribly pompous), what advice would I offer my young friends? Simply this:

First of all, revel in your strengths. You have plenty of them. The stronger you are, chances are, you will be more tolerant. Weakness breeds intolerance. And heaven knows, our world needs tolerance. In 1893, whilst speaking at the World Conference of Religions, Swami Vivekananda said, 'Bigotry, and its horrible descendant, fanaticism, have long possessed this beautiful earth. They have filled the world with violence, drenched it with human blood, destroyed civilizations and sent whole nations to despair.' If that was true in 1893, how much truer is it today?

The Beatles were perhaps prophetic, when they sang 'All You Need Is Love'. India celebrates diversity; in diversity lies strength. Take that message to the world.

Be committed to honesty and integrity. They are the two most faithful friends you can ever have. You might find them wanting when it comes to short-term gains but in the long run, you could not ask for more staunch allies. Stand up for what you believe in. There is nothing more despicable than a 'fence-sitter'.

Set the highest standards for yourself. My (late) father always used to say, 'If a job is worth doing, it is worth doing well, or not at all.' Believe me, it works. In fact, I would like to take this advice a step further and say: 'Be passionate about what you do, for it is only then that you find true self-realization.'

Let me illustrate with a deeply personal example. In 2005, I was hospitalized with a multi-organ failure. My heart, liver and kidneys had been badly compromised and I lay in a semi-coma for nearly three months. As it happened, I also underwent my fourteenth heart surgery at the time. Later, when I was recuperating, many friends and well-wishers came to me and asked, 'Do you really want to head a school anymore? After all, it is such a demanding job.'

I thought about what they said, but the answer was very clear to me. It was not the heart that worried me. After all, medical science had invented the pacemaker that can look after the heart. It is the soul that I was concerned about. Do I have the soul for the job? And what is the pacemaker for the soul? It's one's passion for the job. I figured that if I could get up every morning and say to myself, 'What a great day! And what a great opportunity to do something new or differently, or to touch someone's life'—I had my pacemaker for the soul. Take this passion with you. Believe me, you will be a winner each time.

Learn to reach out to others. One of the things you will realize about life as you get older is that there is a much greater and a much purer joy to be had from giving, rather than from receiving. Ask any mother. The world today agonizes about 'human rights'. Strangely enough, no one seems to be speaking of 'human duties'. It seems to me that if everyone performed their genuine 'human duties', we would spare ourselves a great deal of agony about 'human rights'.

And finally, never lose the child in you. The most delightful thing about a child is its laughter. Don't ever forget how to laugh—particularly at yourself. And, let your eyes light up with child-like glee at the prospect of a challenge. As a child, when you saw a tree, you wanted to climb it. Life will present you with many such trees. You can either seek solace in the shade, or try to get to the top and get a commanding view. Remember, too, that a child's great virtue is its spontaneity. Learn to be spontaneous and genuine in your relationships.

And what do we look forward to from our students? We look forward to their leading us to the Promised Land—the land so famously described by Nobel laureate Rabindranath Tagore (which I have taken the liberty of paraphrasing slightly), when he wrote:

> *Where the mind is without fear, and the head is held high*
> *Where knowledge is free*
> *Where the world has not been broken into fragments by narrow domestic walls*
> *Where words come out from the depth of truth*
> *Where tireless striving stretches its arms towards perfection*
> *Where the clear stream of reason has not lost its way in the dreary desert sand of dead habit*
> *Where the mind is led forward by thee into ever widening thought and action, into that Heaven of freedom, my father, let this generation lead our Brave New World*

Acknowledgements

I would like to thank my family for all the support they have provided me, not only in the writing of this book, but indeed all through my career.

My grateful thanks to my dear friend, Kalyan Ganguly and my old students from Hyderabad House, Doon school, without whose help much of what has happened around the book would not have been possible.